Classic Restaurants

OF

MONTGOMERY

Classic Restaurants

OF

MONTGOMERY

KARREN PELL AND CAROLE KING

AMERICAN PALATE

Published by American Palate
A Division of The History Press
Charleston, SC
www.historypress.com

ISBN 9781540243713

Library of Congress Control Number: 2020930475

Notice: The information in this book is true and complete to the best of our knowledge. It is offered without guarantee on the part of the authors or The History Press. The authors and The History Press disclaim all liability in connection with the use of this book.

We dedicate this book to our research angels,
James Fuller and Martin McCaffery.

Contents

Contents

Acknowledgements

Writing *Classic Restaurants of Montgomery* was quite a ride. We learned a lot, worked a lot, researched a lot and got a lot of help. The following people put up with us when they were busy and helped us when they were probably tired of hearing from us. Much of our thanks go to Dr. Richard Bailey for sharing his immense amount of knowledge. We have a bunch of appreciation for Jeff Benton for his amazing work that we used profusely. We have huge amounts of gratitude for James Fuller, Betty Pouncey and Pat Clark at the Montgomery County Historical Society, who allowed us to use their resources, and we would like to especially thank James for sharing his personal knowledge. Bro Krift at the *Montgomery Advertiser* was gracious and generous in allowing us to use the newspaper's photographs. Martin McCaffery is personally responsible for a large amount of this book's content, as he sent us a lot of newspaper articles on different restaurants. Sandra Polizos met us for lunch, graciously returned our numerous telephone calls and led us through the Greek chapter. Marilyn Lehners Dries met us for coffee, and her stories and photographs of Pont Rouge were indispensable to the chapter. Our friend and neighbor Carol Mosely connected us to Dot Moore and Mary Elizabeth Furnald; all three ladies provided us with amazing information and photos. Our thanks go to Ruth Ott for clearing up "Monkey Sprinkles," and other interesting tidbits. Our thanks also go to Emily Blejwas, her fabulous book *The Story of Alabama in Fourteen Foods* and to Annie Crenshaw for her knowledge and the information in her book *Southern Traditions Cookbook*. We would like to give our thanks to

ACKNOWLEDGEMENTS

Danna Cofer, Scott Smith and Cindy Myers Reynolds for perservering and helping us find a photo of Pop Myers Popcorn. Running a restaurant is hard work, but several proprietors and managers were amazingly helpful to us. Big thanks go to Bryan Trammell at the Vintage Year, who, after helping us with the book for thirty minutes, personally made Karren a reservation for "Burger Night." More of our thanks go to Martha Hawkins, who talked with me at her amazing restaurant and was kind and gracious. (Oh, and check out Martha's for some of the best catfish *ever*.) Carole and I had a great time hanging out at the counter with Theo and Gus at Chris' Hot Dogs. I loved that Gus shared his bottle cap collection. A special nod of our appreciation goes to our new best friends Gay, Hunter and Angela Harrison at Hamburger King. Our thanks also go to Lisa Harrison, who kept the rescue kittens so work could be finished. Our thanks go to Tricia Crowley for being on chauffer duty and helping with photographs. Finally, our thanks go to Tim Henderson, who ran errands and fixed dinner so we could work on that last big push!

Two Hundred Years of Classic Restaurants

In the 1700s, Alabama was part of the "Southwest Territory," or land that was still occupied by various Native American tribes; so, white settlers moved into Alabama later than other states that were above the Alabama–Georgia border. Andrew Jackson defeated the Creek Confederacy at Horseshoe Bend, Alabama, in 1814, and this defeat made huge tracts of land available for white settlement and signaled the eventual departure of the Creek Confederacy from what we know today as the Deep South.

Entire families made their way into Alabama, seeking opportunity, wealth and adventure. Regardless of whether they were poor farmers looking for land, wealthy planters moving to create new plantations or merchants planning to provide services, they all had to be fed. Some traveled light and lived off the land, but others stopped, even while Native American tribes still occupied the territory, at trading posts and taverns that offered simple fare in well-traveled areas. Before Montgomery's founding, the area was an established destination, and food and drink were available to its visitors. Vickers' Tavern, built in 1818, was a log cabin fenced with pine rails on the corner of what is now Dexter Avenue and Decatur Street. Travelers could get a room and food there for only three dollars a day.

Montgomery was created when two villages that were settled beside each other, New Philadelphia and East Alabama Town, merged. Just before Alabama achieved statehood in December 1819, the Alabama Territorial Legislature named the merged communities Montgomery. The new city was named after Revolutionary War hero General Richard Montgomery, who

Alexander Faim's Tavern is pictured in this 1847 painting, which is often listed as the oldest painting of Montgomery. *Courtesy of the Alabama Department of Archives and History and the Landmarks Foundation.*

died during the American assault of Quebec. Montgomery became a rowdy frontier town composed of forty-nine frame buildings; there were no schools or churches, but patrons found food and drink in three taverns. Across the street from Vickers' Tavern, the Globe (also known by the more romantic name of the Indian Queen) opened in 1820, and in the same year, Freeny's welcomed guests at the corner of Commerce and Tallapoosa Streets.

In 1846, Montgomery became Alabama's capital. The city's persona shifted to include politics along with commerce and, according to historian Mary Ann Neeley, "began to assume a more sophisticated air."[1] Although most of the city's socializing and eating took place in private homes, Montgomery's downtown area had several establishments that offered food and drink. By that time, the dining hall in Montgomery Hall was fully operating.

In 1861, Alabama seceded from the Union, and Montgomery was designated as the capital of the Confederate States of America. The

Confederate cabinet stayed in the Exchange Hotel; its members conducted many meetings there and certainly dined in the Exchange's dining room. When the Civil War ended, although Montgomery had been surrendered and occupied, the city did not suffer any extensive damage. The restaurant at the Exchange Hotel continued to be a popular spot.

The Reconstruction years caused Montgomery to become a rather sleepy town. Racial segregation remained the norm, and many establishments also separated men and women. By the 1880s, a measure of prosperity had returned to Montgomery, and downtown Montgomery's commerce encouraged socializing. Fleming's on Court Street had been in business before the Civil War and continued to be a popular establishment for years after.

The turn of the century brought change to Montgomery, as it was the location of Camp Sheridan, a World War I infantry training base. A young soldier named Scott Fitzgerald met his future wife, Zelda Sayre, at a dance in Montgomery. The famous author and his beautiful wife courted in Montgomery and became a famous couple of the Roaring Twenties. An icon of the Jazz Age, Zelda's beloved ice cream shop, Harry's, was located on Dexter Avenue. And Chris' Hot Dogs made its debut in 1917.

The Great Depression did not affect Montgomery as much as other American cities. While commerce and business certainly decreased, Alabama's agriculturally based economy, the military presence at Maxwell Field and the business that was generated by the capital of the state kept Montgomery working. The Green family bravely opened the Green Lantern Restaurant outside the city limits in 1933.

World War II marked the next big change for Montgomery. Thousands of pilots and military students arrived at Maxwell Field and Gunter Field air bases to receive flying instruction. Montgomery Union Station was also a stop for enlisted men and women on their way to other assignments. Although the bases had their own mess halls, the American Red Cross and the Montgomery Junior Chamber of Commerce offered a free canteen hut close to Union Station for all armed service personnel. Local restaurants enjoyed the patronage of the service men and women. The Blue Moon Inn was popular with service personnel.

At the end of World War II and well into the 1950s, the availability of affordable automobiles, increased incomes and the building boom of suburbs inspired a demographic shift outside of downtown Montgomery. Drive-ins, like the Parkmore, and smaller neighborhood restaurants in shopping centers, like Joe's Delicatessen on Fairview Avenue, became destinations for people who went out to eat.

In the 1950s, Montgomery received worldwide attention with the start of the Montgomery Bus Boycott. The boycott, which lasted from December 5, 1955, to December 20, 1956, was a protest of the Montgomery City bus system's treatment of African American passengers. At that point in Montgomery's history, almost all restaurants were segregated, and many did not serve African Americans at all. The African American community had its own series of eateries. White people were not forbidden from eating at these establishments, but they were run and more frequented by members of the African American community. The bus boycott is credited as being the spark of America's Civil Rights Movement, which brought about legislation that made all segregation illegal. In Centennial Hill, Montgomery's historic black neighborhood, the Ben Moore Hotel and Majestic Café were important gathering places, and today, the buildings are important civil rights landmarks.

After the 1960s, Montgomery's downtown area lapsed into a sleepy stage. The construction of the interstate highway did a large amount of damage to downtown and the surrounding neighborhoods. In addition, social attitudes continued to cause a shift away from downtown to suburban areas. The city's downtown area became largely abandoned, and many of its eateries closed. Beyond downtown, smaller, cozy spots, such as Sinclair's in Cloverdale, became popular.

Today, downtown Montgomery is once again alive and vibrant. Revitalization has created a downtown in which all of Montgomery's citizens and its many guests can enjoy themselves. People attend concerts, relax in open-air bars and enjoy dinner on sidewalk patios. Inside bustling restaurants, patrons enjoy contemporary food along with the ambiance of historic buildings that have been renovated.

Montgomery enjoys a glowing present and looks forward to a bright future. Montgomery's restaurants, as they always have, provide businesspeople and state officials with lunch and offer travelers fun and friendly meals. For residents who know the local spots, the city's choices include juicy hamburgers at the family-owned Hamburger King and crispy fried chicken and other homestyle foods at Martha's Place and Martin's. Keeping up with the times, the Vintage Year in Cloverdale offers an award-winning blended burger along with other dinner choices.

We hope you enjoy this book about Montgomery's restaurants and that you simultaneously take the time to enjoy Montgomery's history and its stories as they are told in *Classic Restaurants of Montgomery*.

Downtown

FROM THE VERY START:
EAT, DRINK AND BE MERRY

Montgomery was formed in 1819 from the consolidation of two villages, New Philadelphia and East Alabama Town. New Philadelphia, founded by Andrew Dexter, was laid out in a grid pattern with north–south streets named for heroes of the War of 1812 and east–west streets named for presidents. East Alabama Town, founded by John Scott, oriented its streets toward the Alabama River and then named them after early settlers and functions, such as Commerce Street, and Native American names, such as Tallapoosa Street. The two towns were joined at what was then and now known as Court Square. The Alabama Territorial Legislature was drawing up plans for entering the Union when the leaders of the settlement petitioned to be recognized as one town. Officials of the new settlement decided to name it Montgomery, in honor of Revolutionary War hero General Richard Montgomery; General Montgomery died in the Battle of Quebec and was the first American general to die in battle during the American Revolution. The petition from Montgomery's officials was accepted, and on December 3, 1819, the city of Montgomery was established. Eleven days later, Alabama became the twenty-second state to be admitted into the United States.

From the time of Montgomery's settlement, the area around downtown's fountain has been known as Court Square. Although the fountain was not constructed until 1885, the combination of an artesian well and the county courthouse created an area that was bustling with business. Buying, selling and watering stock made the area incredibly busy. Although the county

In this shot of the Fleming's bar area, note the cabinet of bottles with a wide assortment of alcohol, and on the other side of the room, notice the sign above the cash register that reads "Fresh Buttermilk—Ice Cold." *Courtesy of the Landmarks Foundation.*

government buildings now reside at Washington Avenue and Lawrence Street—and there is no stock in need of watering—the fountain and the buildings around it remain known as Court Square. As historian Mary Ann Neeley writes: "Even though the courthouse is no longer on the site and the area is not truly square, it will forever be Court Square."[2] Court Square has been and remains the heart of the city.

In the early days, East Alabama's settlers built more homes than businesses, while New Philadelphia boasted a variety of businesses. The businesses in New Philadelphia were located along what was then known as Market Street (it later became Dexter Avenue). Prime real estate for new businesses was close to the area that defined Court Square. However, even before the capitol building was built upon it, Goat Hill, named for Andrew Dexter's goats that grazed there, was also a prosperous area for businesses. Andrew Dexter, who was confident in Montgomery's potential, donated the hill for the future capitol. As the new town grew, new businesses and new restaurants filled in the space between Goat Hill and Court Square. In addition, since

1846, Montgomery has been both the county seat and the state capital, and legislators and other government workers have contributed to the vitality of the downtown area, including its restaurants.

Through Montgomery's two hundred years of history, its eating establishments have included taverns with room and board, large hotels with formal dining rooms, small cafés, lunchrooms and cafeterias. From 1860, the Montgomery Theatre's productions attracted prosperous crowds who often dined before and after shows. World War I soldiers at Camp Sheridan and World War II service personnel at Maxwell flight school enjoyed free canteens, but they also enjoyed a variety of restaurants downtown. Tom Connor, in his popular *Montgomery Advertiser* column, wrote that "right after World War II, there were about fifty eating places within a five-block radius of Court Square, and most of them stayed open all night." Connor specifically recalled New Year's Eve celebrations, when "people of all ages, when midnight approached, headed for downtown Montgomery, where cars circled the fountain, blowing their horns, and church bells pealed, and pedestrians spilled over into the streets forming long Congo lines." After the new year was suitably welcomed, revelers could gather at the restaurants for the first meal of the new year.

The downtown area is considered to include everything from Dexter Avenue and Court Square to the capitol building and the adjoining streets within a reasonable distance. Court Square and Dexter Avenue have witnessed some of the most dramatic moments of American history: the formation of the Confederacy, the order to fire on Fort Sumter, Rosa Parks's refusal to relinquish her seat on the Montgomery city bus, the Montgomery Bus Boycott and the civil rights march from Selma. Downtown has hosted speeches by presidents, homecomings for the soldiers of three wars and a variety of pageants and parades. The area's stores and restaurants have gone through booms and busts. In Montgomery's downtown restaurants, John Wilkes Booth drank himself to madness, Jefferson Davis worked on drafts of secession and Zelda Fitzgerald hailed her "Jellies."

Currently, downtown is enjoying a period of revitalization. Hotels and restaurants welcome travelers from all over the world to Montgomery. Dining options range from pizza to fine dining, from chain to individual restaurants and from new eateries to the oldest eating establishment in Montgomery. In the vibrant heart of Montgomery, people gather, and where people gather, there is always a demand for food and drink. As an 1860 advertisement for the saloon Hole in the Wall, Jr. encouraged, "Eat, Drink and be Merry!"

AMERICAN RED CROSS CANTEEN HUT

Soldiers and Sailors Welcome

The Canteen Huts were not public restaurants, but they played an important role in Montgomery's history. They provided food and beverages, free of charge for military service personnel in downtown Montgomery, during both world wars. The Canteen Huts were known as the Junior Chamber of Commerce Free Canteen and were operated by the Red Cross Canteen Corps.

In World War I, from 1917 to 1918, the canteen was located on Lee Street, close to Union Station. A sign on the building read "Montgomery wishes to honor and serve our returning soldiers and sailors." Mrs. Leon Weil organized "The Hut"; in addition to providing food, beverages and the ever-popular cigarettes, the Hut was a place for the troops to rest and enjoy a bit of socialization.

During World War II, the free canteen opened in October 1943, on Commerce Street, and was built on the site of the Windsor Hotel. John West, who, at the time, resided in Boston, made the site available. Local historian John Hawkins Napier III noted that in April 1943:

> *Major General Ralph Royce, commanding the U.S. Army Air Forces Southeastern Flying Training Command headquarters at Maxwell Field, wrote Mrs. Fred S. Ball Jr., American Red Cross Canteen Corps chairman, suggesting that a canteen be set up at Union Station for troops passing through by train. W.A. "Bill" Leavell led the Montgomery Jaycees in co-sponsoring the project with Mrs. Ball's group.*[3]

Former Jaycee member Hugh Stuart worked hard to help the canteen become a reality, right up until he became Private Hugh Stuart with the marines. As he was served the first cup of coffee from the canteen, on the day he was leaving for bootcamp in San Diego, California, he told a *Montgomery Advertiser* reporter, " I have been waiting for this cup of coffee for a long time, and it makes me feel a great deal of pride in my city to be able to receive it before I leave for active duty."[4]

Mrs. Ball and her deputy, Mrs. Charles R. Bricken, opened the canteen with forty-five volunteers. The canteen was later operated by over two hundred female civilian volunteers who had taken courses in nutrition and food service. They wore Red Cross uniforms and worked four-hour shifts,

The ladies who ran the canteen in World War I. *Courtesy of the Ball-Matthews Collection and the Landmarks Foundation.*

keeping the canteen open from 7:00 a.m. to 11:00 p.m., seven days a week. On Saturdays, the canteen often stayed open well past midnight, as trains brought service personnel through Montgomery late into the night.

"The Hut," as it was locally known, offered food, beverages and cigarettes to service personnel and their families free of charge, and it was open to all service personnel, regardless of gender or race. The Hut was located close to the train station, because servicemen passing through Montgomery, who were often traveling with their families on their way to their designated military camp, were short on time and cash. Service personnel would learn quickly about the Hut from signs in the train station; they were able to go there, load up on sandwiches, coffee and cigarettes, and get back to the train on time.

It is impressive that the food was donated—coffee, iced tea, sandwiches, doughnuts and cookies were always available. Sometimes, even more substantial food, such as soup and chili, was also served. The masons

Above: African American soldiers were welcome to enjoy Cokes, smokes and coffee at the "Hut" during World War II. Note train shed in background. *Courtesy of the Ball-Matthews Collection and the Landmarks Foundation.*

Left: Soldiers and sailors could enjoy both a smoke and a cup of coffee at the "Hut" during World War II. *Courtesy of the Ball-Matthews Collection and the Landmarks Foundation.*

regularly provided fried chicken, and the USO provided support; but the bulk of food, beverages and even cigarettes and magazines were donated by Montgomery citizens and businesses. In a *Montgomery Advertiser* article, a spokesperson said that, if every citizen and business that contributed had been listed, it would have taken an entire page.

Napier wrote that, during World War II, the Hut served three-quarter of a million service personnel—men and women. He also noted that international servicemen and women were served at the Hut, including "at least one German Afrika Korps POW accompanied by a U.S. Army M.P."[5] On Christmas 1943, the canteen served two thousand full dinners.

Service personnel would often leave mementoes at the Hut. They also would pick up postcards that featured the Hut, which they would then send to friends and relatives across the United States, telling them about Montgomery's hospitality. Letters that were sent to the Hut from service personnel (later published by the *Montgomery Advertiser*) show that the Hut provided a much needed and appreciated service.

In August 1945—the last month of World War II—the Canteen served a record of forty thousand uniformed people. After two-and-a half years of service, the American Red Cross Canteen closed on April 13, 1946.

BASTIANNI AND CASSIMUS CANDY KITCHEN AND ICE CREAM PARLOR

In his popular *Montgomery Advertiser* column titled, "Remember When," Tom Connor described the Bastianni and Cassimus Candy Kitchen and Ice Cream Parlor's building as unusually large for an ice cream parlor, with a "light and airy décor that you'd expect to find in a turn-of-the-century emporium of a much larger city." Both the Bastianni and Cassimus families were Corsican. The establishment was a favorite meeting place, located near the present site of Kress on Dexter Avenue.

Bastianni and Cassimus must have had several locations on Dexter Avenue, including a site that was "snuggled under the stairs leading to the second floor of the Winter Building," and the stores did not always sell ice cream. A notice dated October 18, 1905, and headlined "Something To Eat," in the *Montgomery Advertiser* promoted "the Bastianna and Cassimus Restaurant" as offering "the best the market affords." In an advertisement in the *Montgomery Advertiser*, dated May 15, 1909, Dave Fleming announced that

In this 1900 photo, Cassimus Candy and Fruit is noted as being located at 124 Dexter. *Courtesy of the Landmarks Foundation.*

he had purchased the business Bastianni and Cassimus and moved it to 10 Dexter Avenue. Fleming stated that "the entire building will be remodeled and renovated. The front part of the building will be changed entirely." Fleming had exciting plans for his new establishment:

> *During the summer, I will sell the best soft drinks, ice cream and confections to be found in the South. Prompt and polite service. Pure and fancy ice cream, made fresh daily and delivered to any part of the city. Quarts, half gallons, gallons and larger quantities.*
> *—Dave Fleming, proprietor*

While this *Montgomery Advertiser* announcement from Dave Fleming is dated 1909, Connor wrote that the establishment closed "prior to World War II."

THE DUTCH HOUSE

The Dutch House had two locations: 315 Montgomery Street, where the Rosa Parks Museum is now located, and 45 Commerce Street. Many Montgomery residents can recall being taken there to eat as children and

The Dutch House on the corner of Montgomery and Molton Streets. *Courtesy of the Landmarks Foundation.*

spinning around on the stools at the lunch counter. In the late 1980s, the Dutch House on Montgomery Street was a favorite of the town's late-night crowd. The staff of the all-night radio station WKLH FM 92, whose studio was on the fifth floor of the Whitley Hotel, jokingly called the Dutch House the "Ptomaine palace."[6] This derogatory term did not stop the radio disc jockeys from being frequent guests of the establishment, devouring cheeseburgers in the early morning hours. For other late-night guests who were out and about, doing more partying than working, the last stop of a fun-filled night was always the Dutch House, where they would enjoy coffee and lemon meringue pie. The Dutch House closed in the 1990s.

THE RENAISSANCE HOTEL EXCHANGE BAR

Ignite the Night

The Renaissance Hotel Exchange Bar, located in downtown Montgomery at 201 Tallapoosa Street, is connected to the Renaissance Hotel and Spa. In reality, the bar is two bars: a small cozy bar inside and a large outdoor patio bar outside. The Exchange Bar stands at the former site of Freeny's Tavern. Freeny's bell, on loan from the Alabama Department of Archives and History, is preserved and protected in a glass case inside the Renaissance Bar, named Freeny's Bell Tavern at the Exchange in honor of the original establishment. Outside, on the patio, a replica of the bell stands proudly on a high stand. In the original Freeny's Tavern, the bell was rung to signal that the workday was over and that it was time to indulge in libations. Linking to that history, the current bar offers daily drink specials called "bell ringers," and the bartender can ring the bell at will. The other part of the bar's name, "the Exchange," honors two historic hotels, the old Exchange Hotel (1846–1905) and the second Exchange Hotel (1906–1974), that stood on Court Square and functioned as the social centers of Montgomery until the second one's demolition in 1974.

During the cold months at the Renaissance Hotel Exchange Patio Bar, heavy plastic is hung from the roof and tall space heaters keep the winter cold out and the merrymaking in. The bar's comfortable, contemporary furnishings allow guests to relax and enjoy "signature cocktails," with names like the "Blackberry Shine" and "Tallapoosa Punch." The menu also offers "Alabama inspired" appetizers that include regional favorites, like Conecuh sausage dip, Creole pasta and its signature dish, gulf jumbo crab cake with a homemade tartar sauce. In addition to its entrées and drinks, the bar offers a cigar menu and often features special nights that tempt with "a flight of a featured cigar flavor." If all of this was not enough, the popular spot hosts live music every night, featuring the area's talent.

THE EXCHANGE HOTEL DINING ROOM

The Modern Hostelry of the South

The Renaissance Hotel Exchange Bar, located in downtown Montgomery at 201 Tallapoosa Street, is named after the gone-but-not-forgotten, historic

Right: A replication of the original Freeny's bell stands at the Exchange Bar. *Author's collection.*

Below: Tourists and residents enjoy the outdoor atmosphere at the Exchange Bar. *Author's collection.*

Exchange Hotels. The first Exchange Hotel was a four-story brick structure that was designed in the Greek Revival style. Matthew Blue wrote that it was built in a time when "a mania for hotel building seized the capitalists…for the growing wants of the community and the influx of strangers during the sessions of the general assembly."[7] The hotel's architect was Samuel Holt, and it was built in 1846 and 1847 by contractors Robinson and Bardwell. The hotel was opened in 1847 by J.J. Stewart; among its amenities was a fine dining room. In September 1852, Washington Tilley took over the management of the hotel after Stewart retired due to his failing health. Blue continued to say that, in 1855, Sterling Lanier and sons took over for Tilley; Sterling Lanier was the poet Sidney Lanier's paternal grandfather. Sidney Lanier and his younger brother, Clifford, both worked as clerks at the hotel. Local lore says that when Sidney Lanier, who was both musician and poet, was working as the night clerk, "he brought all the music and romance of his soul into this old hotel."[8] The story goes that hotel guests were often wakened in the middle of the night by strains of music. After rising and "stealing from their bedrooms, they would join a crowd in the rotunda who were, in place of being irritable from having sleep disturbed, happily listening while Sidney Lanier played his flute in the office, oblivious to his spell-bound audience."[9] During the last years of the Civil War, the Exchange Hotel was run by Bulger, Hukill and Co., and after the war, the hotel was operated by Abram Watt.

In an editorial comment of her collection titled *The Works of Matthew Blue*, Mary Ann Neeley wrote that "the grand Exchange Hotel was the social, business and political gathering spot of the town."[10] When the first capitol building was burned in 1849, the state legislature held its meetings in the Exchange's dining room. The Old Exchange Hotel is historically notable, as it housed the Confederate Congress that met in Montgomery and elected Jefferson Davis as president of the Confederate States of America. The order to fire on Fort Sumter—the action that is considered to have been the start of the Civil War—was issued from the Old Exchange Hotel. Due to the amount of government activity in the hotel's lobby, the Exchange Hotel became known as the unofficial capitol of the Confederacy. Its dining room was likely the main public place where Confederate politicians dined. Despite the hotel's popularity, William Howard Russell, correspondent for the *Times* (London), considered his dinner at the Exchange Hotel of "roasted squirrel and baked opossum" a "gastronomical disaster."[11]

Along with the Confederate Congress, Jefferson Davis and his wife, Varina, stayed in the Exchange Hotel before their house was ready. Historian

The
Exchange Hotel

"*The Modern Hostelry
of the South*"

Your Patronage

is solicited with the assurance of prompt and courteous attention. Comfortable rooms and southern cooking that is unsurpassed.

The Dining Hall is on the Mezzanine Floor and the Lunch Room adjoins the lobby on the main floor.

The traveling public will find the management ready to serve you at any time.

Exchange Hotel

JOHN MOFFATT, Manager.

Below: The first Exchange Hotel's balcony was a perfect spot for presidents and other dignitaries to address a crowd. *Courtesy of the Landmarks Foundation.*

Right: An advertisement that targeted the "traveling public" promised southern food in both the dining hall and lunch room. *Courtesy of the Landmarks Foundation.*

The second Exchange Hotel continued the popularity of the first Exchange Hotel until the 1970s, when life downtown started to wane. *Courtesy of the Landmarks Foundation.*

Jeff Benton noted that Jefferson Davis was introduced to the public as president of the Confederacy from the balcony of the Exchange Hotel; his inauguration parade left from the Exchange Hotel, and thirty-two years later, his funeral procession left from the Exchange Hotel.

At the end of the Civil War, Montgomery surrendered but was only occupied by federal troops for two days. Historian William Rogers wrote that, during those two days, Captain Charles Hinricks of the Tenth Missouri Cavalry took a walk around downtown Montgomery, and when he noticed the Exchange Hotel, he was told that Jefferson Davis stayed there. Rogers continued to say that Hinricks "made it a point to take a meal in the dining room."[12] In addition to Confederate president Jefferson Davis, United States president Grover Cleveland spoke from the Exchange Hotel's balcony when he visited Montgomery in 1887.

The *Montgomery City Directories* from 1880 to 1898 include advertisements for the Women's Exchange Café, the Exchange Bar and the Manhattan Café. In 1905, the owners tore down the old Exchange Hotel and, in its place, built the new Exchange Hotel, which also featured a fine dining room. The new Exchange Hotel and its dining room continued to serve as the social and political hub of Montgomery until it closed in 1974.

FLEMING'S AND YUNG'S

The Leading First Class Restaurant of the City

Historian Jeff Benton describes Fleming's restaurant as a "Montgomery landmark."[13] In his popular *Montgomery Advertiser* column "Remember When," Tom Connor praised the establishment: "All during the 1890s, and for a decade afterwards, no place between Charleston and New Orleans was so renowned for exquisite dining than Fleming's Restaurant." Connor continued to say that the fine restaurant was "operated by portly Mr. Dave Fleming," and that the "posh Victorian drapery and gas chandeliered establishment catered to the well-to-do from the city and the prosperous planters all over the area." Fleming's is credited with serving the first imported oysters to the city and "several Montgomerians still talk of having to conjure up a lot of nerve to gulp down the first raw one." The oysters, lobsters and other saltwater fish were transported from Mobile Bay, upriver to Montgomery.

Some confusion still exists as to Fleming's name. Some advertisements read "Fleming's" while others read "Yung's," and the public used the names interchangeably. The restaurant's proprietors are listed as John A. Young (his name is alternately spelled "Yung") and David Fleming. Both gentlemen were proprietors; Yung died in 1873.

Fleming's was located at 26 North Court Street, several doors down from Klein and Son's corner. That location was in the center of the street bustle caused by pedestrian traffic to and from the Montgomery Theatre. An interesting note is that, in its early days, Fleming's asked its gentlemen clientele to use the ground-floor entrance, marked "For Men Only," where the bar attracted a lively business. An outside staircase to the second floor was designated "For Ladies Only." An advertisement for Fleming's gave directions to the separate entrances. The advertisement also declared that the restaurant was "The Leading First-Class Restaurant For The City" and enticingly declared that the restaurant served "everything conceivable to eat, served in a way that would tickle the palate of the most fastidious epicure."

Fleming's close proximity to the Montgomery Theatre made it a perfect place for after-show gatherings. Many famous and, indeed, infamous actors and artists performed at the Montgomery Theatre. Perhaps the most recognizable today were the Booth brothers—Edwin and John Wilkes. In late 1860, John Wilkes Booth made his Montgomery debut in R.L. Shiel's tragedy *The Apostate*. He also performed the roles of Hamlet, Richard II

The bar area of Fleming's showed off brass rails and polished mirrors. Note the scroll work that divides the bar and dining room. *Courtesy of the Landmarks Foundation.*

and Romeo at the Montgomery Theatre. During many of his stays in Montgomery, John Wilkes Booth was a popular dinner companion. When writing about that history, "many years after Booth had committed his mad deed," Captain Ashurst commented that there was always a "coterie of young men who were always glad to have Booth as a dinner companion.[14] In spite of his eccentricities and weaknesses, Booth was the favorite of the entire company."[15]

Ashurst went on to tell of an incident at a champagne dinner at Fleming's ior to the start of the Civil War that was an example "of the powers of in Wilkes Booth."[16] Ashurst described the gathering as a "lively dinner," re "the wine flowed freely" and the guests were enjoying themselves the point of exhilaration—even singing and making speeches."[17] John es Booth, however, "as was his frequent custom, sat moody and silent… ed in melancholy."[18] After a while, the young men began to clamor n to join in their folic—chanting his name repeatedly. Ashurst's story es to say that Booth "rose from his seat, with his eyes flashing in rt of inspiration."[19] Booth was intoxicated to the point that he had to hold on to the edge of the table, but that did not stop him from his design. Ashurst described Booth's response to the young men's demand for him to join in their frivolity:

> *He threw back his long black hair, and with his pale face turned upward, he recited "The Lord's Prayer." He did nothing else; he said nothing else. He merely recited "The Lord's Prayer." The effect of his power and elocution was amazing. That crowd...was hushed into silence before he had uttered three words. Before the roll of that wonderfully modulated voice, vibrant it seemed, with every tender feeling had ceased, every man about that table, including myself, was weeping. When he finished John Wilkes Booth never noticed his triumph over that dinner party but dropped to his seat and, with his head on the table, covered his face with his hands.*[20]

Fleming's continued to be a favorite spot for dinners before and after performances at the Montgomery Theatre—and for other celebratory times—after the Civil War and during the days of Reconstruction.

The dining room of Fleming's featured tables with white linen cloths and waiters who were ready to serve. Note the ornate heating stove and wall stenciling. *Courtesy of the Landmarks Foundation.*

One advertisement in the *Montgomery City Directory* exclaimed that the establishment was "Open Day and Night." The advertisement adds to the confusion over the restaurant's name, as it is titled "Young's Restaurant" and lists "David Fleming, Proprietor." The text states, "This old reliable restaurant still continues open for the accommodation of the public. Polite attendance, and the table supplied with the best the market affords."

On January 5, 1905, a *Montgomery Times* newspaper article described a remodeling of the Fleming's dining room that replaced the "old time somberness with bright walls and light and warmth color" that made the interior "modern." Nonetheless, the writer said, in a nostalgic manner, "In the olden days of the city, the frequenters of the place were gentlemen of prestige and ladies of fashion." In addition to leisure dining, the restaurant was a place for the influential to meet: "Many a state's campaign was outlined over the wine and cigars." Nevertheless, the writer maintained that the menu remained "as delicious, service as excellent and the appointments as well ordered" and that Fleming's "will always be as it is now, a place to enjoy a perfect meal perfectly prepared." Fleming's closed shortly before World War I, and David Fleming died in 1918.

FREENY'S TAVERN

Major Clement Freeny built his tavern in downtown Montgomery in 1821. Freeny's Tavern was Montgomery's first brick building; the bricks were handmade and the wood hand-hewn. At that time, the tavern was the only building large enough to host important entertainment events. Montgomery's first historian, Matthew Blue, stated that it was ninety feet long and sixty feet wide, with two stories and a double verandah that circled the entire structure. Also known as the Montgomery Hotel and the Bell Tavern, Freeny's provided sleeping accommodations, food and beverages. The bell, as tradition holds, was rung every day at 5:00 p.m. to proclaim the end of the working day and to announce that it was time for libations, inspiring its name as the Bell Tavern. An 1821 announcement in the *Montgomery Republican* proclaimes that the "large and commodious house is now finished and ready for the reception and accommodation of travelers." The advertisement continues to say that "all the exertions in the power of the subscriber [Freeny] shall be made to render it comfortable." In addition to "private rooms with good fireplaces," the advertisement promises that Freeny's "bar will be constantly

The original
Freeny's bell.
Author's collection.

supplied with the best liquors." Lastly, human travelers were not the only considerations: "[Freeny's] stables are commodious and well-constructed and provided with an excellent hostler."

Matthew Blue maintained that the new village, while having a rough frontier exterior, had a more cultured side. Blue stated that a thespian society was formed in 1822: "The dramatic talent among early inhabitants was soon developed."[21] The town's first theatrical performance was produced on December 17, 1822, at Freeny's Tavern—Blue called it the Montgomery Hotel. The production was of William Shakespeare's *Julius Caesar* and featured many of the town's leading citizens.

The second floor of the tavern was also the site of a grand ball that was given in honor of the Revolutionary War hero and the last surviving French major general of the American Revolution, General Gilbert Motier Marquis de Lafayette, when he visited Montgomery on Sunday, April 3, 1825, and stayed through midnight on Monday, April 4. His visit commemorated the fiftieth anniversary of American independence. Tales are still told about the furniture, carpeting and dinnerware that was brought from private homes to the tavern to make the interior suitable for a guest so esteemed as General Lafayette. The bell was rung in Lafayette's honor, and Mary Ann Neeley, Montgomery's favorite historian, wrote that the ball was "one of the first stellar events that took place in Montgomery" and that the ladies of the town dug out their wedding dresses to wear to the event.[22] For years afterward, the women of Montgomery told their daughters and granddaughters of how they danced with Lafayette. In fact, Mary Ann Neeley's great-great grandmother was among those honored by a turn around the dance floor with the hero of the American Revolution. In addition to the memories of dresses and dances, it seems that the ceiling was so low that some of the taller gentlemen, including Lafayette, had to bend over to dance, but that detail is often lost in the memory of that event. Historian William H. Brantley of Birmingham described the event further:

> *The New Orleans Band charmed the assembled guests with both martial and ballroom music. It was a glamorous occasion, flavored with excitement, as it joined together in this frontier village the show and polish of French nobility with the strength and directness of pioneer democracy. The memory of this event will never perish in Montgomery.*[23]

Indeed, to this day, a bronze plaque stands in commemoration of the event. The historical marker, a bronze plate embedded in granite, was erected in 1905 by the Sons of the Revolution on the southwest corner of Tallapoosa and Commerce Streets. The marker was removed in 2003 due to the remodeling of the civic center. However, the Montgomery chapter tracked the marker down and had it reinstated at the original corner, where Freeny's Tavern had stood—currently the site of the Renaissance Hotel. On April 19, 2014, the Montgomery Chapter of the Sons of the Revolution re-dedicated the marker; chapter members stood at attention in period dress uniform, and historian Mary Ann Neeley, representatives from the mayor's office and Renaissance Hotel general manager Walker Stevenson were also present. Compatriot Charles Bruce Pickette, the primary member responsible for the event, was recognized for his efforts. The plaque reads as follows:

> *On this site stood, until 1899, the house in which Marquis De Lafayette was given a public reception and ball, April 4, 1825, while on his last tour throughout the United States. This tablet, placed by the Society of the Sons of the Revolution in the state Of Alabama in lasting memory of this illustrious patriot and soldier of the Revolution, the friend of Washington and the youthful champion of liberty. April 4, 1825–April 4, 1905.*

However, one unfortunate event did take place. A member of the New Orleans band hired for the ball given in Lafayette's honor, Joseph Toussant, arrived on April 3, 1825—ahead of Lafayette's arrival. He and Reuben Green Bates fought, and Bates stabbed Toussant. Dr. Charles Lucas tried to save Toussant, but he died. Historian Matthew Blue states that Lucus's fee and Toussant's shroud and burial expenses (he was buried in Montgomery) were billed to the state as part of the expenses of hosting Lafayette in Montgomery.[24]

On January 1, 1878, *The Weekly Advertiser* recounted the (hopefully) only time that a rat was dined upon in Montgomery. The story goes that "a party of gentlemen" were sitting by a cheerful wood fire in the office, when a good-sized rat passed near enough to have his hair singed. Although the rat was fast enough to spare himself a serious burn, he was not able to save himself from the quick maneuver of General Thomas S. Woodward, who "secured him by the back of the head." The tale continues that Woodward held a loan against one of his companions sitting by the fire. Woodward offered to mark the loan paid if "he would make a meal of the rat." The loan must have been extensive, because the merchant accepted the opportunity, and "in a short while, there was nothing left of the animal—not a bone, a piece of the hide nor even a claw." However much the merchant's finances were improved, his reputation in Montgomery was seriously tarnished. The tale was retold until, at last, "the rat-eater was so twitted about the singular and unnatural performance that he removed to New Orleans," where he encountered more socially acceptable good fortune and became quite wealthy.

Freeny's Tavern remained a staple of Montgomery social life for many years. Clement Freeny died in July 1838. A photo dated 1898 shows that the door at the corner of the building led to the Charles Brady Salon. A *Montgomery Advertiser* article published on June 4, 1900, bemoans the tearing down of the building:

> *The famous old Lafayette building (aka Freeney's Tavern) on Commerce Street is being torn down. One of the oldest in the state—it was here that General Lafayette was entertained in his triumphant tour of the country in 1825. A handsome $30,000 building will be erected at once. A number of people were at the building yesterday, gathering bricks as souvenirs.*

However, some portion of the building must have remained, as historian Wayne Flynt noted that it was destroyed by a fire in 1926. Today, the building is gone, but the memories of the grand Lafayette ball remain, as does the bell.

Freeny's Tavern, built in 1824, provided travelers with a place to sleep and travelers and residents alike with a place to enjoy libations. *Courtesy of the Art Works Collection.*

A historic recipe for Lafayette Ginger Cake can be found in Annie Hadden Crenshaw's beautiful family compilation of history, lore and recipes titled *Southern Traditions: Recipes and Reminiscences from Seven Generations of the Crenshaw Family.* This recipe is from the collection of Elmira Caroline Womack Crenshaw (1832–1867); the collection is dated 1852, and she called it a "Receipt Book." The Crenshaw family was living in Butler County when Lafayette visited Montgomery. Annie Crenshaw noted that her ancestor, Judge Anderson Crenshaw, made no note in his diary of participating in any of the activities honoring Lafayette. Nonetheless, this recipe was passed down. Family tradition holds that the recipe originated from George Washington's mother, who supposedly prepared this gingerbread for General Lafayette when he visited the Washington family in Virginia in 1784. Since the treat was widely popular and often made, it is not too much of a supposition to think that it was served at Freeny's Tavern on that memorable night.

Crenshaw provided notes that lead modern readers to have an appreciation of the effort that cooks went through in this time period. Crenshaw explained that "'molasses, or 'long-sweeting' was an American vernacular preference over the British word 'treacle,' representing a syrup made from boiled sugars." Pearlash was "literally wood ashes from the fireplace or refined 'post ash' used as leavening." As Crenshaw explained, all ovens in this time period used wood; they were either wood stoves or ovens built into the side of a masonry fireplace. Therefore, a quick oven was one with a hot, fast-burning fire and the oven's interior temperature, or heat, was mid-high to high.[25]

Lafayette Ginger Cake

1 ½ pounds of wheat flour
¼ pound of butter
1 pint of molasses
1 pint of sugar
10 eggs
Ginger to taste
1 teaspoon of pearlash dissolved in warm water

Stir in together and bake in pans or patties. Currants and raisins may be added. A quick oven is required for this cake.

HARRY'S CIGAR AND SODA SHOP

Meet Me at Harry's

Harry's soda fountain and short order restaurant, owned and operated by Harry Arrington, stood on Commerce Street. Harry's was a very popular place right before World War I and remained popular until the Great Depression; a common slogan of the restaurant was "Meet me at Harry's." The front doors folded back, and the entire front of the establishment opened to the street—like a Paris sidewalk café.

The block surrounding Harry's hosted a variety of establishments that attracted a good deal of pedestrian traffic. On one corner, the Exchange Hotel reigned, and on the other was the Gay-Teague Hotel. Along the street, May's Pool Hall, a shooting gallery, a couple of men's shops and the Pickwick Café attracted young men who liked to gather, shoot pool, drink coffee and, in today's vernacular, "see and been seen."

According to Tom Connor in his popular *Montgomery Advertiser* column "Remember When," the area became known as the "Jelly-Bean Beat," referring to a slang term for the young men. The term was not entirely complimentary, as a "jelly-bean" was a young man who dressed in stylish clothes to make an impression on young women. However, regardless of how these young men might have "dressed to impress," many were missing

Zelda (a Montgomery native) and Scott Fitzgerald both found inspiration at Harry's. *Courtesy of the Landmarks Foundation.*

other important attributes, such as intelligence and education. In Montgomery, they loitered about Harry's, flirting with girls who walked by; some of these girls even came in and joined the jelly-beans in enjoying milkshakes and other snacks. A favorite of the ladies was the buttermilk shake, made from homemade buttermilk in an ice cream freezer.

Regardless of the rather negative reputations of the "jellies," Connor maintained that Harry's was "something special." Aside from its location and reputation as a roosting place for the jellies, Connor explained that it was "a legend for its home-churned ice cream and… [Harry's] wife's famous cakes."

Harry's was popular because of its good food, and it was a fun place to eat. The walls were mirrored and marked off into boxes. When the radio announced the score of a baseball or football game, some jelly-bean would mark it on the mirrored wall, and the whole place would erupt in cheers or sounds of disappointment. Connor finally said, "To top it all off, young Harry Arrington featured Montgomery's first drive-in service." The carhops were a "colorful bunch," with names like "Snake, Scorpion and Leaping Jesus," inspired by New York writer Damon Runyon's characters.

A *Montgomery Times* article dated July 2, 1921, recounted an interesting event that involved Alabama's blue laws and Harry's. Blue laws, also known as Sunday closing laws, make selling or opening certain businesses on Sunday illegal, in observance of the Christian day of rest and worship. In Montgomery, an exception was made for restaurants; Harry maintained that he owned a restaurant license for both the city and the county. The prosecution maintained that owning a license did not equate to owning a restaurant. Harry argued that, despite his restaurant's reputation of being a place where young people socialized and drank milkshakes, 80 percent of his business's profits came from the drinks and sandwiches that were eaten there. Judge J. Winter Thorington (another well-known Montgomery name) agreed with Harry and dismissed the case. Other well-known Montgomery restaurateurs (as the good judge decided they, indeed, were) included T.S. Turk of Turk's and A. Franco of Franco's.

Famous Jazz Age couple Zelda and F. Scott Fitzgerald were at least a fringe part of Harry's scene. According to an oft-repeated Montgomery story, before her marriage to writer F. Scott Fitzgerald, Zelda Sayre liked to ride down the street in front of Harry's in a convertible. When the boys would yell to her, she would laugh and call them "all her jellies." F. Scott Fitzgerald's short story "The Jelly-Bean" was inspired by the young men.

Harry's closed at the start of the Great Depression but re-opened in the new Shepherd building after about ten years. The Shepherd building was designed by Montgomery's most-established architect of modern skyscrapers, Frederick Ausfeld, and was built in 1922 at 312 Montgomery Street. In addition to Harry's, the Shepherd building was home to doctors, insurance companies and real estate agents. The Shepherd building was donated to Troy University in 2002 and was listed in the National Register of Historic Places on May 22, 1986, until it was demolished in November 2010. Harry's enjoyed several years of prosperity at the Shepherd building; however, it was the Harry's at the Commerce Street location during the Roaring Twenties and World War I that F. Scott and Zelda Fitzgerald made Harry's famous.

HOLE IN THE WALL, JR.

Eat, Drink and Be Merry

The Hole in the Wall, Jr. Saloon was located on the ground floor of the Montgomery Theatre at the corner of North Perry and Monroe Streets. The theater occupied the second and third floors and opened on October 14, 1860. The post office and various other businesses were located on the ground floor, including the Hole in the Wall, Jr. saloon and restaurant.

A *Montgomery Advertiser* newspaper announcement declared that the Hole in the Wall, Jr. would open on November 13, 1860. The advertisement boasted that the establishment offered patrons "The Best of Everything" and advised them to "Eat, Drink, and Be Merry!" One last description claimed that the establishment was "An Excellent Restaurant, a splendid Saloon and the Best Cigars." The Hole in the Wall, Jr. was operated by Joseph A. Diaz along with Tom Williamson & Company.

Indeed, the Hole in the Wall, Jr. held good on its claims as indicated in a *Montgomery Daily Mail* article: "A good and happy time was had on Saturday

The building in the foreground of this photograph is the Montgomery Theatre. The theater, closed in 1907, housed Webber's Department Store for many years (note sign). The building collapsed during renovation in 2017. *Courtesy of the Landmarks Foundation.*

night." The article continued with a brief description of the establishment: "It is very neat…not gaudily arranged." The article ended with the observance that those present "had a good old time."

It is not known when Hole in the Wall, Jr. closed, but the Montgomery Theatre closed on November 13, 1907.

JEFFERSON DAVIS HOTEL DINING ROOM

Montgomery's Finest

The Jefferson Davis Hotel was built in 1927 at 344 Montgomery Street and was named after the president of the Confederate States of America. The hotel was a stately landmark and one of Alabama's finest hotels. At the height of its popularity, it offered 250 modern guest rooms that were all air conditioned and each room had a television. The hotel also hosted the WSFA radio station studio, where Hank Williams was a popular guest in the 1930s. The Jefferson Davis Hotel remained segregated until the 1960s. However, the WSFA radio station allowed African American preachers,

Above: This postcard promotes the Jefferson Davis Hotel's informal lounge and more formal dining room. *Courtesy of the Landmarks Foundation.*

Left: The Jefferson Davis Hotel's dining room menu cover capitalized on Montgomery's Civil War history. *Courtesy of the Montgomery County Historical Society.*

including Ralph David Abernathy and Martin Luther King Jr., into its studios to broadcast sermons on Sunday mornings.

The attractive Urban Room was a fine-dining restaurant and a popular feature of the hotel. The hotel also welcomed guests to the Surf Lounge, including Scott and Zelda Fitzgerald and Clark Gable. The hotel's dining room menu was large, and the cover featured a profile of Confederate president Jefferson Davis and the White House of the Confederacy—the house where Davis and his wife lived while Montgomery served as the capital of the Confederacy. The entrées list began with appetizers that included the ever-popular oysters, but at the Urban Room, oysters were served with sherry. The specialty of the house was steak; options included strip sirloin, a "Ladies" sirloin and filet mignon. The hotel also offered grilled sugar-cured ham steak, prime rib of beef, Chinese dishes—chicken chow mein and chicken chop suey—and Italian spaghetti with meatballs. The menu offered a variety of seafood, including red snapper, salmon, flounder, trout, crab, shrimp and oyster stew. Desserts ran from an elegant creme de menthe parfait to a southern favorite—Sweet Potato Pie. The menu also included a more era-specific dish—fruit Jell-O!

The Jefferson Davis Hotel was added to the National Register of Historic Places on March 13, 1979. The building has been renovated and currently offers ninety-eight apartment units for seniors and persons with disabilities.

KRESS LUNCH COUNTER

The World's Best Vegetable Soup

Samuel H. Kress built the first Kress store in downtown Montgomery in 1898. The Montgomery store that now stands on Dexter Avenue was designed by George E. Mackay in 1929, and it is noted by historian Jeff Benton as one of the "most elaborate" of all the Kress stores in the United States.[26]

The first Kress store in Montgomery burned and was demolished. During the construction of the new store on the same site, the basement walls collapsed, ruining the entirety of the new construction and damaging several adjacent buildings. The current store's design was inspired by Samuel Kress's interest in preserving ancient buildings. In the 1920s, the king of

The Kress Department Store faces Dexter Avenue in this streetscape. Kress is the sixth building down from the H.L. Green store and is next to Baker's Shoes. *Courtesy of the Landmarks Foundation.*

Italy knighted Kress for his contributions toward saving Italy's ancient buildings. One of the buildings Kress had assisted in preserving was the Temple of Hera in southern Italy. The design of the Kress store's façade was inspired by and includes many elements of the Temple of Hera and the classic Doric style. The building is an entire block deep; one entrance faces Dexter Avenue, and the second faces Monroe Street.

Mrs. Murille Holt Gunter was the Kress lunch counter manager from 1934 to 1960. The menu offered "the world's best vegetable soup" for the cost of five cents—or seven cents with fresh corn muffins. Other favorite menu items included pork chops, ham, fried chicken, chicken and dumplings, collards, turnips and black-eyed peas. The counter's homemade pies and cakes included Lane cake, fruit nut pudding and, on Tuesdays, Pillsbury lemon pie.

The *Encyclopedia of Alabama* states that Lane Cake is an established southern dessert, and Alabama is credited with its origins. Emma Ryland Lane of Clayton, Alabama, won first prize at the county fair in Columbus, Georgia, for her cake, which she called "The Prize Cake." In 1898, she published a cookbook titled *A Few Good Things to Eat*. The recipe proved to be very popular, and she was persuaded to name it after herself. The cake is four layers, with filling between each and a white frosting on the top and sides. It is known for its bourbon or brandy filling. Lane Cake is even mentioned in

Harper Lee's beloved novel *To Kill a Mockingbird*. In the book, Scout Finch's neighbor is known for her Lane Cake recipe, which she guards ferociously. She bakes a cake for Scout's aunt Alexandra when she moves in with the Finch family. Scout gets a little tipsy from her piece of cake: "Miss Maudie Atkinson baked a Lane Cake so loaded with shinny it made me tight." In 2016, Lane Cake was made the official dessert of Alabama.[27] The following recipe is titled "Lane Cake: 1898 County Fair Winning Recipe," but it makes some changes for the modern kitchen. For example, the original instructions said to seed and finely chop raisins (today most raisins are seedless), and this recipe asks for pans to be lined with waxed paper, while the original said to use brown paper. Also, the original recipe measured the boubon as "one wine glass of good whiskey!"

Lane Cake

*Make a day or two before serving to allow
the filling's ingredients to blend.*

*3¼ cups sifted cake flour
2 teaspoons double-acting baking powder
½ teaspoon salt
1 cup butter
2 cups sugar
1 cup milk
1 teaspoon vanilla
8 egg whites*

Preheat oven to 375 degrees Fahrenheit. Put wax paper in the bottom of four nine-inch cake pans. Sift together flour, baking powder and salt. In a large mixing bowl, cream butter, and gradually add sugar, mixing well until light and fluffy. Combine dry ingredients with the creamed ingredients gradually while adding milk as you go. Mix together well, and add vanilla while mixing. Separate the egg yolks from egg whites and save the yolks to use in the filling. Beat egg whites with an electric mixer in a separate glass bowl until soft peaks form. Gently add the beaten egg whites to the cake batter. Be careful not to overmix. The batter will be smooth but will look slightly granular. Divide the batter evenly into the four pans. Bake in 375-degree oven until the edges shrink slightly away from the sides of the pan and the cake tester or toothpick inserted in center of each layer comes out clean—approximately 20 minutes. Place pans to cool on wire racks for 5 to 10 minutes. Turn the layers out of the pans, onto wire cooking racks; remove the waxed paper and turn the layers right-side-up. Cool completely.

Filling
8 egg yolks
1 ½ cups sugar
½ cup butter, room temperature
1 cup seedless raisins, finely chopped
1 cup pecans, chopped
1 cup bourbon or brandy
1 teaspoon vanilla

Beat egg yolks well. Add sugar and butter to the egg yolks and continue to mix well. Put in a two-quart sauce pan and cook over medium heat, stirring constantly, until thick—15 to 20 minutes. When thickened, remove from heat. Stir in raisins, pecans, bourbon and vanilla. Cool slightly, and then spread generously between each cake layer.[28]

The Kress Lunch Counter offered counter and table service. The kitchen was located at the rear of store, in the basement. During the Jim Crow era, eating facilities were racially segregated; and like other establishments, Kress only allowed its African American customers to enter through the Monroe Street entrance—they were not allowed to eat at the lunch counter. Through a back door on the lower level, a very small snack bar was operated for African Americans.

The Kress building closed in 1997, and the building sat empty for many years before it became an important part of Montgomery's downtown renewal. It opened to fanfare in 2018 as a newly renovated and redesigned building that offers first-floor retail and upper-level residential units. An important part of the building's renovation included the preservation of two marble slabs that, in the past, had been a part of the segregated public water fountains—one is marked "white" and the other is marked "colored." A *Montgomery Advertiser* article quoted developer Mark Buller on the decision he made to include architectural elements of Kress's segregated past in the design for the present: "Rather than downplay it, we decided to feature it and let people talk about the differences and how much better things are today."

LEE'S GRILL

According to Tom Connor in his popular *Montgomery Advertiser* newspaper column "Remember When," Lee's Grill was one of "Montgomery's most popular restaurants and coffee-break meeting places." Owned and operated by Lee Pake, the small grill was located in downtown on Commerce Street. Connor described it as "not so very wide but seeming to reach nearly through the block to North Court."

Despite the fact that the building was narrow, its patrons felt it was big enough for them. Connor continued, "Its appeal was its convivial, yet cosmopolitan aura that catered to coffee cliques of railroad men, bankers, investment brokers and politicians." The close proximity of the patrons gave "the place the flavor of a livestock auction and the New York Stock Exchange combined." Lee's Grill's popularity lasted until after World War II.

LOUISE'S SNACK BAR

Louise's Snack Bar was located in the Old Tyson building, across from the *Montgomery Advertiser's* location from the 1940s to the 1960s. Owner and operator Louise Pickens, later Louise McKay, was as popular as her snacks. Louise could not see, but she never let that slow her down or dampen her enthusiasm. In addition to her own popular personality, her little dog had its own fans. According to Tom Connor in his popular *Montgomery Advertiser* column "Remember When," there was "no more pleasant spot to visit in all Montgomery than Louise's Snack Bar."

METROPOLITAN CAFÉ

According to an announcement in the *Montgomery Advertiser*, the Metropolitan Café was opened on February 2, 1921, at 11:00 a.m. in the Exchange Hotel building on 11 Commerce Street. The announcement promised "polite and quick service." However, the focus of the announcement seemed to be on sanitation, as the establishment emphasized that "above all, strict sanitation" was an important element. Later in the announcement, the theme continued with a promise that the food would be "served in a cleanly manner from a kitchen scrupulously clean."

Promising customers an excellent level of cleanliness was a real marketing plus, as health inspections and grades of sanitation were not yet enforced. A city ordinance in 1850 forbid hotels, restaurants and private dwellings from tossing waste into the streets. Writing about the city streets almost fifty years later, Tom Connor explained that downtown's odors were numerous and of a wide variety—from the odors of fish markets and stables to restaurants and bakeries. In the days before air conditioning, restaurants kept their kitchen doors open and "you could get a good idea of their daily offerings while still a block away."

When doors were left open, odors—pleasant or otherwise—were not the only sanitation issue in the early 1920s. On August 8, 1912, the *Montgomery Times* printed an article regarding a restaurant inspection by city commissioner Walter R. Brussel, head of the department of sanitation and health. The article presents information from the inspections with a certain "tone" that makes the reader think that perhaps the journalist is not an advocate of restaurant inspections. The article states that City Commissioner Brassell:

> *…began this morning a disastrous inspection of all restaurants and public eating places and establishments where food is prepared and served which it is believed will result disastrously for all concerns, and proprietors who are not complying with recently adopted restaurant ordinances governing their sanitary maintenance.*[29]

The writer continued by informing the public that "the commissioner will doubtless be engaged in his inspection tour of restaurants the remainder of this week. Commissioner Brassell will doubtless publish and score the restaurants and places inspected at the conclusion of his round."[30] The consequences for not meeting set sanitary guidelines were strict and clear: "All places not complying with the law and are found to be dirty and

The Metropolitan Café was in the second Exchange Hotel on Court Square. *Courtesy of the Landmarks Foundation.*

unsanitary and will be prosecuted…on warrants issued at the instance of the commissioner." Evidently, some discussion concerning the sanitary guidelines and the need for inspections had been ongoing. The writer declared that Commissioner Brassell "was vehement in his declaration that the laws would be enforced" and went on to add that the enforcement was guaranteed to be "without fear or favor." It seems that the commissioner felt that he had been "threatening prosecution and arrests too long" and that things had come to the place where there would be no further leniency shown to anyone.[31]

Ron Dawsey from the Montgomery Health Department Alabama Department of Health stated that state health officer Samuel W. Welch, MD, submitted the annual report for the Alabama State Department of Health for the two-year period, from January 1, 1919, to December 31, 1920, that is most likely the beginning of a standard inspection program. In the annual report, Welch made several observations: the Bureau of Investigation was charged with "the maintenance of sanitary conditions in the hotels, barbershops, eating establishments, soda founts and like places in the state."[32] Welch noted that, in 1920, some of the bureau's challenges included the "short period since the establishment of the bureau, the great extent of the field of work and the territory to be covered and the lack of personnel. This report consists of a presentation of the situation and of plans and policies for the year 1920."[33] Welch maintained that restaurant inspections were needed, along with a standard of "physical equipment and methods employed."[34] Welch also gave a specific example that said, "The washing of glasses at soda founts is frequently so seldom or so carelessly performed as to be a mere pretense."[35] He added that, "regulation is needed in the production and distribution of clean milk and other dairy products, the manufacture of carbonated drinks under hygiene conditions, the distribution of wholesome meat products and such other problems of sanitation, as may arise, are matters which will receive the attention of the bureau during 1920."[36]

Welch had a positive attitude about the future of sanitary inspections and regulations, even if the process had just begun. Welch stated that inspector C.A. Abele "has met with hearty cooperation."[37] Nonetheless, Welch continued by saying, "We recently got out a bulletin in which the regulations governing hotels, restaurants and barbershops were printed. This is a very interesting issue of the State Board of Health Bulletin, and it is to be hoped it did not find its way to the waste basket when it visited your offices."[38] Hopefully, since Montgomery restaurants had been meeting inspection guidelines since 1912, the state inspections did not present that much of a change. From the emphasis on cleanliness and sanitation in the advertisement, the public must have considered meeting health standards as a desirable element in a restaurant.

Aside from a high level of sanitation, other information that was included in the Metropolitan Café's advertisement was that its manager was Sam Minas and that it would be "open day and night." The advertisement also provided information on cost efficiency: "Bring a meal ticket—$6.00 meal for $5.00." The café also served a "Special Sunday Dinner." The menu included relishes, such as Apalachicola oyster cocktail, and soups, such as Cinnamon Croton. The café's entrées included spring lamb and roast young chicken. For dessert, guests could choose between vanilla ice cream or lady fingers (a pastry), and drinks included sweet milk and buttermilk. The Metropolitan Café is now closed.

MONTGOMERY HALL

In 1831, George Whitman created a company to build Montgomery Hall, a hotel, on the southwest corner of Lawrence and Market Streets (now Dexter Avenue). The contractor, John Crane, finished the building in three years. Historian Matthew Blue stated that "the original cost of the lots and building was fifty thousand dollars."[39] Benjamin Wilson and John Bluck opened Montgomery Hall for business in the fall of 1835.

Montgomery Hall is notable to historians on two counts. The most mentioned is the fact that, when Montgomery served as the capital of the Confederacy, Montgomery Hall housed many of the Confederate legislators. But a more active event from 1835 was recorded by Montgomery's first historian, Matthew Blue, when he wrote in his diary about a knife fight at Montgomery Hall. Montgomery, in its early days, was a rowdy frontier town, and the knife fight serves as an example of some of the violence its citizens endured and were eventually able to stop. It seems that the altercation was incited by the political division between Democratic and Whig party advocates. Democrats Kenyon and William Mooney sought revenge on Whigs Bush and Edward Bell. The men attacked each other with knives in a "desperate and bloody battle."[40] Bush Bell killed William Mooney on the spot, and Kenyon Mooney fatally wounded Edward Bell.

Regardless of its association with street violence, Montgomery Hall maintained an excellent reputation. At its height, it could house 150 guests, and its restaurant impressed many travelers who were accustomed to larger cities and establishments. Montgomery Hall's dining room served guests throughout the entirety of the Civil War. The *Montgomery Advertiser* newspaper ran an advertisement for the dining room that stated the bar was well stocked and the restaurant had "ample food" and was able to provide "comfort second to no hotel in the South."[41] During Reconstruction, Montgomery Hall housed federal officials. One story says that the proprietor was asked to pay back taxes; she retorted that she would be able to meet that request if the federal officials paid their rent.

In 1874, the Houston fountain, named in honor of newly elected governor George Smith Houston, was placed in front of Montgomery Hall. By the 1880s, Montgomery Hall was no longer the showcase hotel nor lavish dining room of its previous years. It was later demolished, and the United States courthouse and post office was built in its place.

The Houston Fountain was placed in front of the Montgomery Hall Hotel in 1874. *Courtesy of the Landmarks Foundation.*

NATIONAL LUNCHROOM COMPANY

The National Lunchroom Company was located on North Court Street. As can be seen in the photo on the following page, the "colored entrance" was clearly marked. What cannot be seen in the photograph is the "white entrance," which was on the same side of the building, just a few feet away. Classic southern food was the lunchroom's specialty, as can be seen by the writing on the window, which advertises "fried chicken, fried fish and a breakfast with two eggs for 25 cents."

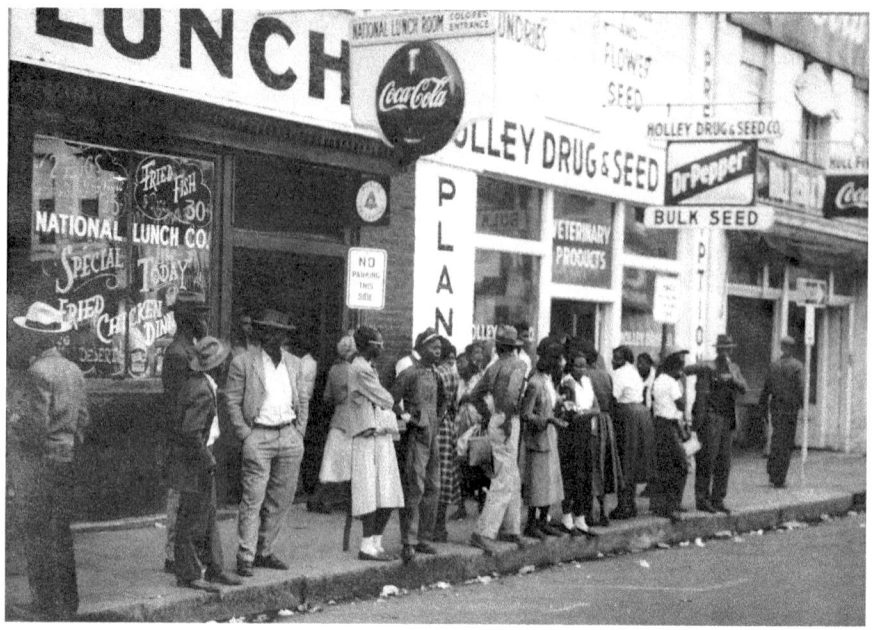

The busy sidewalk outside of the National Lunchroom Company was typical for a Saturday downtown before the late 1950s. *Courtesy of the Landmarks Foundation.*

Georgia Gilmore, known for her contribution to the Montgomery Bus Boycott, worked as the head cook at the National Lunchroom Company until the beginning of the Montgomery Bus Boycott in 1955. The National Lunchroom Company catered to the blue-collar clientele in downtown Montgomery. Gilmore talked about cooking bacon and eggs for breakfast and greens for lunch. She was fired from National Lunchroom Company for testifying in support of Martin Luther King Jr. and other civil rights leaders who were facing charges in regard to the Montgomery Bus Boycott. Such actions were expected, and to spare others her fate, Gilmore founded "The Club from Nowhere" as a shield for people who wanted to support the Montgomery Bus Boycott but could not risk losing a job. It is now closed.

TANGERINE CAFETERIA

The Tangerine Cafeteria was located above the Electric Maid Bakery in Court Square, near the Strand Theatre. Before the establishment became a cafeteria,

The cover of Mary Furnald's novel features an original sketch of the Tangerine Cafeteria by her husband, Donald Furnald. *Courtesy of the Mary Furnald Collection.*

it was a tearoom; and when its new owner, Susie Stowers, took over, she decided to keep the name. Additionally, author Mary Furnald, Stowers's great-niece, remembered that "the entire entrance was painted bright orange. When Susie originally opened the cafeteria, it was already painted that color. Her finances were so strained that she could not afford to repaint it. She had laughingly said, 'I'll just call it The Tangerine Cafeteria."[42] Furnald remembered that everybody loved her aunt.

To visit the Tangerine, as it was informally referred to, a single door on the street opened to a hallway and a flight of stairs. Guests went up the flight of narrow stairs and opened a door at the top. Inside, there was an L-shaped serving counter. Furnald remembered that Stowers always served fruit cocktail. Tom Connor, in his popular *Montgomery Advertiser* column, "Remember When," described the Tangerine as "a meeting place for coffee drinkers all day long." Some of those meetings were between representatives and senators from the Alabama State Legislature. Furnald stated that it was common knowledge that more state business was carried out at the Tangerine than in the capitol building. However, its popularity was most evident at lunch time, as patrons formed long lines to enjoy a midday meal of homestyle meats and vegetables. Tom Connor also mentioned the affordable prices: "No matter how much you ate, it seemed impossible to ever run up a bill over seventy-five cents." Regardless of the prices, cashier Mrs. Snider was there to ring up the bill. The Tangerine Cafeteria closed shortly after the end of World War II.

THE TAVERN CAFÉ AND FRANCO'S RESTAURANT

The Tavern Café was located on the corner of Church and Lee Streets, across the street from the United States post office. In addition to the postal service, the building housed the offices where World War II recruits got their physicals and

This pre–World War II photo shows the establishment called the Tavern Café. *Courtesy of the Landmarks Foundation.*

were inducted into the United States Army. After being inducted, the soldiers were given lunch vouchers. The Tavern, which was actually a café, became the most popular place for the World War II recruits to redeem their vouchers. However, the government did not like the name of the establishment, because it sounded like a bar, and the government did not want to pay for soldiers to eat and drink at a bar. So, the owner changed the name to Franco's, and the lettering on the windows promoted pizza and seafood.

Next door to the Tavern Café, Abraham Franco opened a delicatessen in 1906, and in 1933, Morris Franco opened the Italian café known as Franco's. A *Montgomery Advertiser* promotion from April 24, 1938, referred to the Franco brothers and said that the café was located at the corner of Church and Lee Streets. The advertisement suggested that readers "bring the family down today," and offered a "Special Sunday dinner of roast turkey with dressing and cranberry sauce." The advertisement also noted that a "Special Breakfast [was] served every morning"; the special breakfast included eggs, bacon, grits, rolls, jelly and coffee—all for fifteen cents. In addition to its special breakfasts the Tavern and Franco's had a thriving nightlife. The same advertisement reminded the public that Franco's hosted live music from 7:00 p.m. to 9:30 p.m. every night.

Franco's closed in 1956 after serving the public for sixty-three years, and it was noted in a *Montgomery Advertiser* article. The café's proprietor, Isaac Franco, said that he was "the last of five brothers" and that he had worked there for fifty years.

2.
A City on the Move

In 1886, the Capitol City Street Railway electrified one line of its streetcars. The trolley line, known as the Lightning Route, because it could move six miles an hour going uphill and downhill, was the most influential factor in developing neighborhoods and parks beyond Montgomery's city limits. In 1887, the company made all fifteen miles of its service electrical, making it among the first all-electric public trolley systems in North America. The neighborhoods it fostered were also among the first developments in the South that became known as suburbs. Before the trolley provided service beyond the city limits, most residents lived near the downtown area. Places of employment, stores that supplied needed items and restaurants were all located in the downtown area. Travelers also stayed in hotels and ate in restaurants in the downtown area. The trolley made living, working, shopping and dining in a larger downtown area a reality, and it made living beyond the city limits convenient.

In addition to providing transportation to work and the feasibility of new homes and businesses outside of town, the trolleys were soon used as entertainment vehicles. In the heat of summer, people would ride the trolleys just to take advantage of the breezes that were gained from its movement. Of course, where folks gather, there is always an opportunity for refreshment. According to Tom Connor in his popular *Montgomery Advertiser* column, "Remember When," in the 1920s and 1930s, vendors waited in the High Street area with fried fish for a nickel and "a pile of real bar-b-q for a quarter."

from quick snack-to leisurely
meal--here's food to suit your need

TASTY BURGER $.50
Montgomerys finest Double Decker Hamburger

HASTY CHICKEN $1.00
Chicken in Basket Including Potatoes, Salad, Rolls

CLUB STEAK $1.65

AIR CONDITIONED
Breakfast Served at all Hours-Pancakes
Special Luncheon-Dinner

Open 6 AM-11:30 PM   Federal Drive

Paul's Sugar and Spice Drive-In at 1600 Federal Drive was a popular hangout for teenagers. *Courtesy of the Landmarks Foundation.*

Although the trolleys were popular in their time, they were replaced by automobiles and buses by the late 1930s. The Lightning Route made its last run on March 8, 1936. Restaurants opened on streets beyond Dexter Avenue, but they were still considered downtown restaurants. The suburbs grew and new restaurants opened in Cloverdale and on Madison Avenue, heading toward Capitol Heights. In the early 1950s, restaurants in motels became popular, as did restaurants in areas that were considered country locations. Writer and historian Ruth Ott wrote that:

> *World War II changed the lifestyles of Americans, and Montgomery was no exception. Postwar prosperity allowed more families to buy a second car. Inexpensive gasoline helped fuel the trend. By the 1950s, two-car families were becoming the norm. The trend in business was to create businesses that served people in cars—the drive-in.* [43]

As Montgomery's city limits grew to include more than downtown, families ate in motel dining rooms on their way to vacation spots, teenagers cruised through drive-ins while listening to the radio and the hamburger became an iconic American food. In Montgomery's restaurants beyond downtown, F. Scott Fitzgerald took a break from writing *Tender Is the Night*,

Martin Luther King negotiated with city officials to end the Montgomery Bus Boycott and Elvis ate popcorn. Montgomery was on the move, and as Montgomery grew and changed, so did its restaurants.

ALLEN'S MALTED MILK STAND

Allen's Malted Milk Stand opened in 1941 and faced Madison Avenue at the juncture where Hopper Street now intersects Madison Avenue. Allen's was the predecessor of fancier drive-ins like the Parkmore and Susie's. Some patrons walked and some rode bikes, but those who drove automobiles attracted young women. Milkshakes and hamburgers were sold for a dime at Homer and Juanita Allen's popular eating establishment. Waitresses delivered the food on small trays that could be hooked over car windows. When Hopper Street opened, Allen's moved up Madison Street, to the current location of Earl's Monument Company. Allen's Malted Milk Stand is now closed.

THE BLUE MOON INN

Montgomery's Unique Restaurant

The Blue Moon Inn's name was inspired by the adage, "only once in a blue moon," which refers to the difficulty that one has finding superior food in a unique and attractive setting. The Blue Moon Inn must have met the criteria, as its steady popularity lasted for almost fifty years—from 1919 to 1968.

The Blue Moon Inn was initially owned and operated by Miss Leila Dowe. The restaurant was in a quaint frame cottage that was built around 1840 on 1816 Goode Street (now E.D. Nixon Avenue). The Blue Moon Inn's promotional material provided a story on how the Dowe family acquired the building. Leila Dowe's grandfather, John Dowe, was walking in Court Square in December 1879, when he recognized a friend who was engaged in auctioning property. As Dowe passed by, he raised his hand in greeting. Later that day, to his surprise, his friend told him that his raised hand had been taken to mean that he had placed an offer—and it was accepted. History says that Dowe paid for the property in gold. In addition to the five-room cottage,

Above: The Blue Moon Inn was located at 1523 Goode Street, which is now named E.D. Nixon Avenue. *Courtesy of the Landmarks Foundation.*

Left: In Alabama, everybody knew what to expect when the Blue Moon Inn's advertisement stated "Southern Food." *Courtesy of the Landmarks Foundation.*

the property included twenty acres. Since the cottage was built in the 1840s, it had a kitchen house with a brick floor. Brick floors were standard in the construction of kitchen houses in order to prevent fires. Being separate from the main residence was another precaution. However, the distance between the kitchen house and the cottage of the Blue Moon Inn had been enclosed. The timbers that had been used in the original part of the cottage were hand hewn and joined by wooden pegs. While the original house was well preserved, three wings had been added.

A *Montgomery Advertiser* review stated, "Leisurely dining was enhanced by the homey atmosphere of the old house, with its wide pine boards and high ceilings." The architecture of the historic home was an important part of the restaurant's ambiance in all seasons. The dining rooms were furnished with early American antiques. In summer, guests were served drinks outside where "a fountain [played] on a spacious three terraced garden" enclosed by "old brick walls covered in fig vine and ivy." During the winter months, log fires and the "glow of candlelight provided a cheerful atmosphere." Another feature that made the Blue Moon Inn unique was its absence of a sign.

The *Blue Moon Cookbook* sold through eight printings. *Author's Collection.*

President Franklin Delano Roosevelt dined at the Blue Moon Inn during his visit to Montgomery in 1933. When President Roosevelt was a guest of Alabama governor Miller at the Governor's Mansion, Leila Dowe catered the event. This luncheon took place during the Great Depression, and she always noted that the governor's kitchen was so poorly equipped that she had to bring her own light bulbs. During its heyday, the Blue Moon Inn was considered the perfect location for graduation parties, bridal showers and literary club meetings. Military personnel also frequented the Blue Moon Inn.

From 1968 to 1978, the Blue Moon Inn was owned by Cecil McMillan. McMillan was also the author of the cookbook *Once in a Blue Moon Cookbook*, which was inspired by the Blue Moon Inn's favorite dishes. McMillan graduated from Michigan State University's school of restaurant management before he worked for four years at the Blue Moon Inn. Seafood Belmont, chicken county captain, stuffed squash, poppy seed dressing with fresh fruit and mocha cake were some of the Blue Moon Inn's most popular dishes. The cookbook happily sold through eight printings.

The Blue Moon closed in 1978, and the building was demolished in 1985.

Angel Food Cake (for Mocha Cakes)

1 ½ cups egg whites
1 teaspoon cream of tartar
1 ½ cups sugar
½ teaspoon of salt
1 cup cake flour, sifted twice
1 teaspoon vanilla

In a mixing bowl whip egg whites and salt until foamy. Add cream of tartar and mix until stiff but not dry. Slowly mix in sugar, do not overmix. Add vanilla. Remove bowl from mixer and fold in flour using a wire whip or spatula. Use over and over motions rather than whipping in flour. Pour in an ungreased ten-by-fifteen-by-two-inch pan and bake at 325 degrees Fahrenheit for about an hour or until cake pulls from side of pan and feels done in center. Invert on cake rack and cool before removing from pan. The mixing bowl and cake pan must be absolutely free of any grease.

Mocha Cakes (fifty cakes)

Remove cooled angel food cake from pan. With hands, peel off soft brown crust. Cut cake five times lengthwise and ten times across with a very sharp knife. With a metal spatula, generously ice cakes on four sides and top with mocha icing. Roll in toasted, chopped or coarsely ground peanuts. The cake is much better if you toast large, shelled peanuts. Remove husks by rubbing together and grind just before using. Refrigerate cakes in hot weather. These are good rolled in ground, toasted almonds.

Owners Leila Dowe and Cecil McMillan posed for a formal portrait that was published in the *Blue Moon Cookbook. Author's collection.*

Mocha Icing (for twenty-four cakes)

1-pound box 10X confectioners' sugar
2 sticks butter
1 tablespoon instant coffee

Dissolve coffee in one tablespoon of cool water. Cream butter until light and fluffy. Add sugar in small amounts, beating well after each addition. When half the sugar has been added, mix in small amounts of the coffee alternately with the remaining sugar. Continue beating until very fluffy.

Blue Moon Cheese Sandwiches (Sixteen Sandwiches)

2 cups grated sharp New York State cheddar cheese
½ cup chopped stuffed olives
⅓ cup chili sauce
½ cup chopped pecans
¾ cup mayonnaise
I teaspoon Worcestershire sauce

Mix together well and chill before using. Trim white or whole wheat bread and spread with mixture. Cut into three strips. Refrigerate until serving. I also like to mold this and serve with cocktail crackers.

CORSINO'S

Fine Italian Cuisine Serving Montgomery Since 1954

Corsino's was first opened by Don Corsino and Tony Wilson at 911 South Court Street as Shugar Shack. The grand opening took place on March 20, 1982, and its promotion advertised "homemade Italian dishes" and, of course, "pizza." Later, a name change occurred and Corsino's was opened on December 25, 1983. Don Corsino and Tony Wilson remained the restaurant's proprietors. The promotion also advertised that Corsino's had the "finest Italian lunch and dinner."

The 1954 date that was listed on the menu referred to the time that Don Corsino worked with his father, Sesto Paesano Corsino. Paesano, as he was normally called, worked as an established chef in Montgomery for several decades. Chef Paesano trained both of his sons, Donald and Randall, at his restaurant, Napoli. When Napoli opened, Paesano Corsino took out a full-page advertisement in the *Montgomery Advertiser*; it was later framed and displayed for many years at Napoli, and it was later displayed at Corsino's for many years. Napoli closed around 1966, and Paesano Corsino died in 1970.

Corsino's was known as a family-run restaurant that made its guests feel like family. Donnie's wife, Myra, was the hostess, and the items on its menu included classic Italian fare. The menu's heading read, "Our Famous Spaghetti," and featured a list of Italian spaghetti with meatballs,

Corsino's was a favorite place for pizza and other classic Italian food. *Author's Collection.*

meat sauce, anchovies, Italian sausage, mushrooms, chicken, chicken livers, garlic and oil. Corsino's "Italian Specialties" included ravioli, lasagna, fettuccini alfredo, eggplant and chicken parmigiana and rigatoni. Several veal dishes were listed under the heading "Especially for You" and promised "pure milk fed veal" in Italian spaghetti with veal cutlet, veal and pepper served with spaghetti and veal parmigiana. Of course, pizza was a specialty of Corsino's, and its options offered included cheese, Italian sausage, green pepper, ground beef, pepperoni, anchovies, mushrooms, onions and Corsino's special. The restaurant's fresh salads included antipasta, which was described as containing Genoa salami, mozzarella cheese, pepperoncini peppers, olives, bell peppers, anchovies and tomatoes. Another favorite salad was the Dago, which was tossed salad with black olives, pepperoni, pepperoncini peppers, mozzarella cheese and Italian dressing. The dessert list tempted patrons with cheesecake, cannoli and spumoni ice cream. Some of Corsino's customer comments on social media include "Best meatball sandwiches ever," "one word: eggplant parsesan" and "best pizza ever."

When Corsino's announced it was closing New Year's Eve 2018, several *Montgomery Advertiser* articles covered what the journalists considered as a loss. The restaurant was a family-owned and -operated business. Its owners, Donnie and Myra Corsino, had been in the restaurant business in Montgomery for all of their lives. One article explained, "Corsino's had built a reputation and a loyal customer base over the decades not only because of its pizza and traditional Italian foods, but because of the warm and friendly atmosphere. *Montgomery Advertiser* newspaper reporter Chase N. Allpots lamented, "Forgive me for being awash in Chianti, for I bring sad news." Allpots described Corsino's as a "quirky but comfortable and loveable, longtime family-run restaurant. Corsino's was a place where you could relax and enjoy unpretentious food served by unpretentious people at unpretentious prices."

Donnie and Myra were ready to hang up their chef hats, but other issues were an aging facility and a worrisome location. They sent a message out to their guests: "It has truly been an honor to be part of such a wonderful extended family of friends, and we love you all."

DALE'S PENTHOUSE RESTAURANT

Meet Me at Dale's

The fire that destroyed Dale's Penthouse Restaurant on February 7, 1967, took lives on that cold February night and remains one of the worst fires in Montgomery's history. Although the restaurant was a town favorite, it is the fire that is most remembered. The construction of Dale's Penthouse Restaurant, and the Walter Bragg Apartments that were the restaurant's rooftop home, marked an important time of shifting values in Montgomery. The February 26, 1950 *Montgomery Advertiser* announcement of the construction of the new building echoed the popular sentiments of wanting Montgomery to be part of a modern present, not just a location of the past. The *Montgomery Advertiser* article described the future building as "a sleek, modern addition to Montgomery's skyline [that would] begin moving upward soon." To make the break in architectural-social values even more dramatic, the new ten-

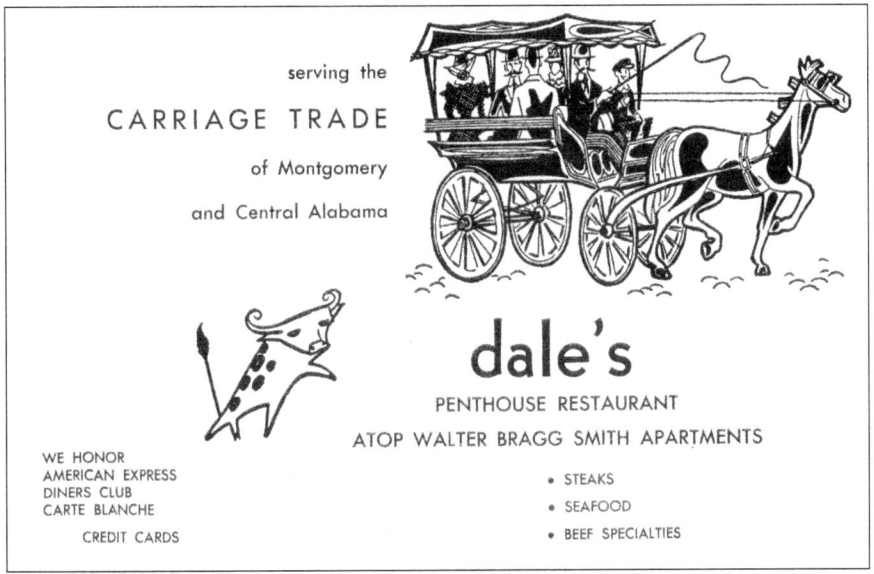

serving the

CARRIAGE TRADE

of Montgomery

and Central Alabama

dale's

PENTHOUSE RESTAURANT

ATOP WALTER BRAGG SMITH APARTMENTS

WE HONOR
AMERICAN EXPRESS
DINERS CLUB
CARTE BLANCHE

CREDIT CARDS

• STEAKS

• SEAFOOD

• BEEF SPECIALTIES

A *Montgomery City Directory* advertisement for Dale's Penthouse Restaurant promoted its steaks, its contemporary welcoming of credit cards and its upscale clientele—known as "Carriage Trade." *Courtesy of the Landmarks Foundation.*

story building was built on the site of an antebellum mansion that had been the home of one of the founders of Montgomery and other notable men who had made their names known in business and retail.

The Walter Bragg Apartments were constructed on the southwest corner of Court and Clayton Streets in 1950; they were within the boundaries of a historic and long-established neighborhood that is still known as Cottage Hill. The *Montgomery Advertiser* published a brief history of the site and stated that the first building on the site was an antebellum home, but its exact construction date is not known. The first documented resident in 1854 was General John Baytop Scott, a son of General John B. Scott and one of the founders of Montgomery. On the eve of the Civil War, Judge and attorney Milton J. Safford sold the house to Mayer Lehman. Lehman owned a dry goods store downtown and was also a cotton factor. The Lehman family lived in the home during the Civil War and for a couple of years afterward (1860–1867).

An 1888 photo notes that, at that time, the home belonged to Joseph Goetter. Goetter ran a popular downtown store, and he later merged business interests with the previous resident of his home, Mayer Lehman. Goetter remained in the home until his death in 1901; his wife stayed in the home until her death in 1902. The home was then purchased by Milton Paul LeGrand. LeGrand died in 1913, but his wife stayed in the house until her death in 1948. After her death, the house, then referred to as the Goetter-LeGrand Home, was sold to various civic organizations that used it for social events, such as antique shows and the popular yearly "Holiday House." The *Montgomery Advertiser* published the wrecking notice of the Goetter-LeGrand home in March 1950.

The announcement of the construction of the new building was published in the February 26, 1950 edition of the *Montgomery Advertiser*, and it presented an exciting description for those wanting modernity: "It will be a $1,000,000, 10-story apartment hotel with a penthouse and a sunroof." The article promised a modern design for the 122 units that featured "continuous bands of glistening glass" circling the building, which provided "maximum light and view." The article concluded by heralding the upcoming building as an "ultra-modern structure—not duplicated anywhere in Alabama."

Dale's Penthouse Restaurant became one of the city's most elegant eating establishments in the 1960s; an advertisement stated that the restaurant was known for "serving the carriage trade"—a term meaning that it served people in the upper economic levels. The advertisement even included a graphic of a horse and carriage with riders dressed in elaborate early 1900s attire. At Dale's in the 1950s, guests dined in the upscale restaurant beside a large window that offered a panoramic view of the downtown skyline. In another *Montgomery Advertiser* article, author Wayne Greenhaw remembered a Friday night happy hour that featured sixty-cent martinis served by popular bartender Ann Harris, and he said that the event attracted many Montgomery notables. "Meet me at Dale's" was both a promotional slogan and a popular invitation, as the restaurant catered to Montgomery's society, the corporate world and government officials.

The menu's signature charcoal-broiled steaks were served with the establishment's own steak sauce—a sauce that is still declared to be the best by those who remember the restaurant. The promotion promised "incomparable foods superbly served." The menu's offerings included a section called "From the Pit"; its choices were extensive and included filet mignon, T-Bone and strip sirloin. Appetizers included broiled chicken livers on toast, and the seafood options included broiled or fried red snapper steaks, Dale's trout almondine and broiled South African lobster tails. The kitchen's specialties were chopped sirloin with a bordelaise sauce or special Penthouse bleu cheese sauce. The desserts that were listed were quite international: apple and cherry pie, French ice creams and sherbets, genuine Italian spumoni and Greek pastry.

The fire that destroyed Dale's Penthouse Restaurant on February 7, 1967, is still considered Montgomery's worst fire. The trauma of the fire remains evident, as the town's media still observes the anniversary of the fire. On the fire's thirtieth anniversary, the *Montgomery Advertiser* published an article headlined "Memories of Tragic 1967 Fire Linger on in Survivors' Minds." According to the *Montgomery Advertiser* article, the restaurant had enjoyed a busy night, and at 9:00 p.m., the staff was winding down and preparing to close at 10:00 p.m. A member of the kitchen staff, Hattie Mae Chappell, remembered that one of the waiters, who had collected a goodly amount of tips that night, had invited his coworkers out for a good time after closing, "The anticipation of an after-work party had put everybody in a good mood." Suddenly, smoke creeped under the kitchen door. An office connected to the kitchen provided access to both the stairs and elevators. Soon, however, the fire stopped the elevators and then cut people off from the stairs—their only option was to break the huge windows.

In the article, Annie Lee Emerson told a harrowing tale of opening a second office door and seeing several boxes of wine; she pulled out one of the wine bottles and knocked out one of the eleventh-story windows that was close to her eye level. Then, she said, "I climbed up on them boxes, got out that window and stepped down on that ledge," referring to the mere two-foot ledge that was eleven stories high and circled the restaurant and the top story of the building. Emerson's tale continued describing how she helped her sister, Betty Ellis: "Betty was behind me. One of her [shoes] fell off her foot, and I helped her out." If their position was not already precarious enough, the smoke turned to flames and, according to the *Montgomery Advertiser* article, "began licking at them from the downtown side."

Around this time, Emerson continued, a young man named Nathan Payman arrived with about six customers, who also climbed out on the now-crowded ledge. Amid the fear and frantic actions, Emerson remembered her friend Jesse Mae Boyd, who was still inside. In a heart-wrenching memory, Emerson recalled, "I was going to help her out. I had her by the hand, but the fire came around, and I had to turn her hand loose." Boyd's body was later found with three others near the office window. By this time, a group of spectators had gathered on the street below and were anxiously watching. To everyone's dismay, those on the ledge and those watching from the sidewalk below, the firemen's ladder could not reach those who were stranded on the ledge. Firefighters were eventually able to clear a path inside the building, from the stairs to the patio, and reach the group, terrified and freezing, on the ledge.

The firemen also had a terrifying experience trying to get to the fire inside the building. They attempted to take the elevator to the tenth floor, but the damaged elevator took them right up to the eleventh floor, where the elevator doors opened to an inferno. The firemen forced the elevator doors closed and prepared to slide down the elevator cables. The other elevator was being operated by the chef, Jesse Williams, who had heroically been getting people to safety. He called to the firemen and said that he was also stuck in the elevator on the eleventh floor. Firefighter J.T. Defee shouted to him that the firemen were going to slide down the elevator cables; Jesse Williams followed them. In the lobby, Defee said that people opened the elevator door so that the firemen and Jesse Williams could climb out.

A total of twenty-five people died in the fire. In addition to those who were with Jesse Mae Boyd, one body was found inside the dining room and another group was sadly clustered on the west end of the restaurant, where there was no escape, as the stairs on the west end

This view of the penthouse after the fire is notable due to the lack of activity. *Courtesy of the Montgomery Advertiser.*

stopped at the tenth floor. The restaurant's hostess, Rose E. Doane, and bartender Ann Harris died while helping people get to safety. The night's casualties included the widely known state politician and former public service commissioner Ed Pepper; his wife, Ann; and Teamster lobbyist Sidney Zagri of Washington, D.C. Wayne Greenhaw said that people were traumatized by the disaster because they had connections to both the place and the people who perished. The *Montgomery Advertiser* article stated that the "twisted wreckage from the fire remained visible atop [what is now] Capitol Towers long after the disaster." Wayne Greenhaw emotionally described the remaining wreckage, "Every time you passed by, the scar was up there in the sky."

This tragedy was compounded by the fact that the deaths were avoidable. Captain Defee told the *Montgomery Advertiser* that if the west side stairs had not stopped at the tenth floor, the customers and kitchen staff could have escaped. Aside from the loss of life and trauma, the consequences of the fire included $60,000 in damages to the building and its contents; employees and customers also filed numerous lawsuits. However, the most positive consequences were the important changes that were made in fire regulations—not just in Montgomery, but on a national level. These changes were initiated to make buildings more fire retardant and to provide escape routes in the case of fire. Today, the building is occupied by the Capitol Towers Apartments.

DANNY'S DINER

We Never Close

Danny's Diner stood at 529 Madison Avenue, at the corner of Madison Avenue and Bainbridge Street. A postcard further states that the diner was one block from the Alabama State Capitol. Owner Danny Long "was a promising young catcher for the Montreal Royals when a play at home plate resulted in a shoulder injury" and an end to his baseball career.[44] While recovering from his injury and wondering what to do with his life, Long started working at a diner in New Jersey. The work inspired him to open a diner of his own. He returned to Montgomery and found an investor. He opened the diner in Montgomery on Thanksgiving Day 1952 and welcomed guests there for fourteen years.

Danny's Diner was housed in one of Montgomery's first modular buildings. *Courtesy of the Alabama Department of Archives and History.*

In his popular *Montgomery Advertiser* column, "Remember When," Tom Connor described Danny's Diner as "one of those places that, from the start, had some intangible quality that immediately caused it to become a gathering place for everybody, from politicians to truck drivers, secretaries to debutantes." The restaurant's staff included Marvin Jackson, the Montgomery resident who invented and produced the world's first attic fan; and Jerry Wilson, a longtime Montgomery waitress "that the whole town knew and loved." Adam Mays, whose background included cooking for some of the city's most distinguished families, "held forth in the kitchen." One of the restaurant's biggest attractions was vice president Annie Mae Long, Danny's "loveable mother," who "reigned at the cash register and made every customer feel like a stockholder in the place!"

The building was a modular design; Danny had ordered the building from a factory in New Jersey. The building was considered the "first modern, restaurant-type diner to begin operation in Alabama." Danny's Diner advertised "We Never Close," and its attractions included late-night baseball stories. Nonetheless, Danny's Diner did close in July 1966.

FARMERS MARKET CAFÉ

Down Home Cooking From Our Family to Yours

In the late 1950s, the original Farmers Market, located at 315 North McDonough Street, was strictly an outlet where farmers could sell their produce. In 1960, as a convenience to the farmers, the Tucker family set up a small counter and two stalls that offered light breakfasts and lunches of sandwiches and camp stew. About five years later, in order to handle the demand, the Tuckers expanded into more stalls, added tables and chairs and opened a cafeteria line. In 1970, as the supermarket chains moved in, farmers began delivering to businesses, but the Tuckers' restaurant became even more popular, so they did a complete turn-around. They renovated the Farmers Market Café to appear as it is today; they left only a few stalls to keep the open-air atmosphere.

In the early 1980s, Phil and Joann Norton purchased the café from the Tucker family. The Nortons served the community for many years with good country cooking, friendliness and a family atmosphere. In 2014, the Burbage family purchased the Farmers Market Café. A statement on their menu declared: "We strive to carry on the Farmers Market Café tradition and continue to make your tummy happy!"

The home-style cooking buffet is popular at lunch. The normal meal comprises a meat and two sides ($8.25) or a meat and three sides ($9.25). A vegetable plate (three vegetables) costs $5 and four vegetables cost $7. The café's various desserts, including pie, cake and a specially made dessert, like Oreo cookie pudding or bread pudding, also tempt hungry guests. Grilled items are also available; a "Grill Market Burger" ($8.00) is described as a "one-third pound of ground beef, grilled to perfection and topped with lettuce, onion and pickles, on a toasted bun." The café's twist on the BLT ($7.50) includes fried green tomatoes, "crispy lettuce and T-Thick cut bacon." The "Farmers Club" ($8.00) features country ham, turkey and thick cut bacon, with American and swiss cheese on toasted bread. A breaded chicken breast on a toasted bun with lettuce and tomatoes sounds good, but guests can "make it buffalo" for $1.00 more.

Although lunch is popular at the Farmers Market Café, breakfast often fills up quickly. The café's usual choices include eggs, grits, hash browns, bacon, sausage, toast and buttermilk biscuits. But the Farmhouse Toast (French toast, $6.00), which is topped with powdered sugar and choice of meat, is also popular. The café's other options include "Country Cakes,"

The Farmers Market Café is bustling on weekdays. *Courtesy of the Crowley Collection.*

which are described as three silver-dollar pancakes with a choice of meat ($6.00); a smothered biscuit, which is actually two buttermilk biscuits covered with country sausage gravy ($5.00); and the "Breakfast Bowl," which is two scrambled eggs with crispy hash browns, sausage and cheese alongside toast or a buttermilk biscuit ($8.00). The breakfast menu also offers a variety of omelets: cheese, farmhouse, Western and veggie; all of them are made with three eggs, peppers, onions, tomatoes and cheese ($7.00).

The dining room offers booths, long tables and smaller round tables. Informally dressed waitresses refill drinks and deliver food orders from the grill. Like they advertise—it's down-home cooking!

THE FRANCIS CAFETERIA

An Atmosphere of Beauty and Quietness

In 1934, Frances Collins Gentry leased the old Weil home on 402 South Lawrence Street to operate a boardinghouse. Gentry later bought the property, and in early 1940, the boardinghouse was replaced by "Frances' Tea Room," which later became "Frances' Cafeteria."

> [Frances Gentry] *commissioned a sign, and the painter mistakenly painted "Francis Cafeteria" [with an "i"], and Frances Gentry decided*

not to change it. "The Francis," as it was known, became synonymous with good food and fellowship. The manager, "Miss Jane" Ellixson, decorated the rooms with fresh flowers and seasonal decorations; ornate stained-glass windows and wooden trim were reminders of a bygone era.[45]

Combined with antique furniture and home-style or "country" cooking, the Francis Cafeteria made its guests feel right at home—or how they would like to feel at home!

A second Francis Cafeteria was opened in 1954 at the new Normandale Shopping Center, and it was managed by Frances Gentry's son, Bob Gentry. In 1957, a third location was opened in Forest Hills Shopping Center. The Normandale branch closed in 1972, and the Forest Hills branch closed in 1977. After Frances Gentry's death in 1979, Bob Gentry and Miss Jane Ellixson took over management at the original location. Bob's wife, Roonie, served as cashier for many years. In 1982, the property was sold to the First Baptist Church, with the stipulation the family could operate the cafeteria as long as they desired. By 1986, the cost of maintaining the facility was prohibitive, and the Francis Cafeteria announced that it would close. The *Alabama Journal* published an article that recognized the Francis Cafeteria's contribution to the city and documented the many recollections that Montgomery's residents had of the cafeteria.

The Francis Cafeteria was located in an elegant old house. *Courtesy of the* Montgomery Advertiser.

Businessmen enjoy their lunch on the Francis Cafeteria's last day in 1981. *Courtesy of the Montgomery Advertiser.*

On the cafeteria's last day of business, the line of guests waiting to get in (seventy-five to one hundred people) stretched down a long series of steps to the South Perry Street sidewalk. The Francis had welcomed guests for fifty-two years—"years that included the Great Depression, where it began as a boardinghouse, and World War II, when it began serving non-boarders." Another employee, who had worked at the Francis for twenty-five years, said that, in addition to loving the work she did at the Francis, she loved to eat at the Francis: "I loved to come and sit in our favorite place (she pointed to a turret shaped corner of the restaurant on the front porch)." Many people still remember Roonie Gentry, Bob Gentry's wife and cashier for over twenty-five years. Other recollections on Facebook include: "Best country fried steak on the planet; tomato aspic with mayonnaise, chopped steak with the little round potatoes and a slice of wonderful custard pie. It was a wonderful part of my childhood; same thing every time: liver and onions, mashed potatoes, brownie pie." One lady declared, "My mother went into labor there—perhaps explains my love of a good buffet!" And the Francis received the best compliment any restaurant can receive: "Would love to be able to eat there one more time."

GEORGIA GILMORE

Like the Red Cross Canteen at Union Station during both world wars, Georgia Gilmore's house was not a licensed, public restaurant. However, the roles that she and the food she prepared played in Montgomery's history are important and deserve to be included in any discussion of Montgomery and its food.

Georgia Teresa Gilmore was described as "kind and motherly," but Gilmore "was also known for her fiery temper, especially in response to the racial injustice so common in 1950s Alabama."[46] Gilmore worked as a midwife until legal restrictions prohibited her from continuing in that profession. She also worked as head cook at the National Lunchroom Company until the Montgomery Bus Boycott started in 1955. The National Lunchroom Company catered to the blue-collar clientele in downtown Montgomery. Gilmore talked about cooking bacon and eggs for breakfast and greens for lunch. She also earned a reputation for her sweet potato pies and fried chicken.

She was fired from National Lunchroom Company for supporting the Montgomery Bus Boycott. In *The Story of Alabama in Fourteen Foods*, Emily Blejwas explained: "Nearly three months into the bus boycott, on February 24, 1956, [Georgia Gilmore] testified in court on behalf of Martin Luther King and eighty-nine other boycott leaders who faced charges of conspiracy."[47] When Gilmore lost her job, she asked Martin Luther King Jr. for advice, and she later reported that he told her, "All these years you've worked for somebody else, now it's time you worked for yourself."[48] King, who was "a fan of her fortitude and her fried chicken," helped her bring her home's kitchen to the point that she could produce the amount of food she needed to help herself and the movement.[49]

Gilmore lived in Montgomery's historic African American neighborhood called Centennial Hill. Centennial Hill was founded soon after the Civil War, during Reconstruction, by freedmen. The neighborhood was anchored by the Swayne Primary School, which was opened in 1867 by the American Missionary Association and the Freedman's Bureau, and the First Congregational Church, which was founded in 1872. The neighborhood took its name from the nation's founding celebrations in 1876. Her home was close to King's home and another meeting place for civil rights leaders, the Ben Moore Hotel and the Majestic Café.

Gilmore started her successful career in cooking by preparing sandwiches, pies and cakes to sell and make money for the Montgomery Improvement

Georgia Gilmore cooked from her house in Centennial Hill. Today, her home is noted by a historical marker. *Author's Collection.*

Association (MIA). The MIA was organized by Montgomery ministers and leaders on December 5, 1955, after Rosa Parks refused to give up her seat to a white man on a Montgomery city bus on December 1, 1955. The African American leaders of Montgomery were prepared for the event of Rosa Park's refusal, and in response to her arrest, they called upon the community for a one-day bus boycott. The information concerning the boycott was spread mainly by word of mouth and fliers distributed by volunteers. The one-day boycott was a huge success, and the MIA decided to continue boycotting the busses until the City of Montgomery made some changes in their segregationist polices of the city bus system.

Martin Luther King Jr., who was, at that time, a young, largely unknown minister of the Dexter Avenue Baptist Church, was the president of the MIA. The bus boycott continued for 382 days and was a stand-off between the MIA and the City of Montgomery. The boycott caused almost empty busses to rattle around their routes, creating reduced income for the city. At first, Gilmore sold her food at the mass meetings of the MIA. The success of that venture led to her selling entire meals, cakes and pies, and she expanded her food's availability to beauty parlors, laundromats and other locations frequented by both bus boycotters and supporters of the movement. Writer John Edge explains, "The group sold fluted pound cakes and sweet potato pies to beauty parlors and laundries, to cab stands and doctor offices. They fried fish and stewed down greens and sold plates of pork chops and rice that mothers and fathers bought and toted home from church to sons and daughters."[50]

As the boycott continued, so did the movement's need for money to pay for gas, car insurance, vehicle maintenance and the other expenses of the boycott and the carpool. Gilmore gathered a group of women to join her in baking cakes and pies to raise money for the MIA and the bus boycott. She later explained her idea, "What we could do best was cook!"[51] She called her group "The Club From Nowhere" in order to protect the other women she cooked with. Gilmore was the only visible officer; therefore, the other women were not at risk of retribution. Writer John Edge explains, "She offered these women, many of whose grandmothers were born into slavery, a way to contribute to the cause that would not raise suspicions of white employers who might fire them from their jobs or white landowners who might evict them from homes they were renting."[52] Her sister, Betty Gilmore, further explained the name: "It was like, 'Where did this money come from?' 'It came from nowhere.'"

In addition to protecting the cooks, according to writer John Edge, the Club From Nowhere created a way that "progressive white Montgomery could support the cause, too, sidestepping the retribution of conservative friends and neighbors by purchasing cakes and pies instead of making outright donations."[53] According to journalist Gingrich:

> *To sustain the community's enthusiasm, the MIA held bi-weekly rallies on Monday and Thursday nights. Gilmore sauntered down the aisle singing "Shine on Me," or "I Dreamt of a City Called Heaven." She then emptied hundreds of dollars' worth of coins and small bills into the collection plate and then announced how much money the Club From Nowhere had collected. In response, the crowded church erupted into a din of applause, stomping feet and a chorus of voices shouting "Amen," and "That's Right."[54]*

The Club From Nowhere inspired other groups, and there was a friendly rivalry. John Edge wrote that "on the west side of town, Inez Ricks of the 'Friendly Club' fried fish and baked cakes."[55] Ricks had testified in court on behalf of the leaders of the MIA along with Gilmore.

But Gilmore did more. In her book *Finding Martha's Place*, restaurateur Martha Hawkins wrote that Gilmore opened her home to anybody in the movement who needed a safe place to eat. Her house was not advertised as a real restaurant, and Gilmore never called it a restaurant. According to Martha Hawkins:

> *Everybody just said they was going down by Georgia's to eat. Reverend King was there often. He needed a place where he could trust the food, and Missus Gilmore supplied. She was known for plating him up with pork chops and bell peppers, and the reverend always asked for a second glass of her famed iced tea. That flavor of what happened inside her walls was what inspired me most. 'Twas something special happening there. The folks writing about Missus Gilmore described meals around her table as more like being a rally than a restaurant. The feeling in her home became downright sacramental, a camp meeting of sorts with a continual loud and loving conversation about the things that mattered. Folks would feel free to stand or sit or walk about from room to room with plates of food in their hands. It was the fact that a person's cooking could become so much more than just cooking—that's what I was aiming to do someday.* [56]

In agreement with Hawkins, John Edge wrote, "In the process, her kitchen became a locus for change." [57]

Gilmore started cooking at 4:30 in the morning; according to writer Emily Blejwas, "Gilmore cooked in cast iron skillets over a regular four-burner stove." [58] By lunch time, folks would be lined up. "Gilmore served the comfort food, or 'soul food' that remains popular today: ham hocks, stuffed pork chops, potato salad, collard greens, candied yams, bread pudding and black-eyed peas." [59] Martin Luther King Jr. loved her fried chicken. Nelson Malden, Martin Luther King's barber, said, "Whenever VIPs would come to town, he [Martin Luther King] would always have Miss Gilmore cook up a batch of chicken." [60] King also loved her famous iced tea.

As the movement grew, other well-known leaders also came to eat at Georgia's house, including Robert F. Kennedy and Lyndon Johnson. Gilmore's son, Mark Gilmore, later said that Johnson and King sat at her twelve-seat oak trestle table that was draped in a white tablecloth and set with hot sauces and peppers and ate deviled eggs served from carnival glass platters. [61] In her book *Feed the Resistance*, writer Julia Turshen stated, "[Georgia's] place was a sanctuary where civil rights strategists could meet safely and in secret."[62] As Reverend Ed Dixon explained, "Dr. Martin Luther King, he needed a place where he could go, where he could not only trust the people around him but trust the food."[63] In an interview, Gilmore explained, in more specific terms, the reason that King's important strategy meetings were conducted at her table: "'Cause so many other places was wired—you know?"[64] So, "throughout the civil rights movement in Montgomery, Dr. King held clandestine meetings around her dining room table, fueled by fried fish and butterbeans."[65]

In an interview many years later, Gilmore explained the idea she had for the restaurant: "See, the way I figured it, people had to eat. So, I made the pies. I made full meals. I'd have two meats every day. I'd have chicken, maybe meatloaf with crème potatoes, cheese and macaroni, rutabagas, peas with okra, lettuce and tomato, apple pie and iced tea."[66] By all accounts, "sitting down to Georgia Gilmore's black-eyed peas and okra and fried chicken was sitting down to Montgomery heaven."[67] In addition to providing safety, comfort and good food, writer Julia Turshen stated, "[Georgia] literally fed the movement. She sustained it."[68]

Georgia Gilmore believed in her cause, in her community and in her own ability to serve both. On March 7, 1990, on the twenty-fifth anniversary of Bloody Sunday and the Selma-to-Montgomery march for voter rights, Georgia got up early to cook macaroni and cheese and fried chicken for those participating in the reenactment; at the age of seventy, she had not been well for some time. The effort of standing and cooking proved to be too much, and she collapsed and died. The food she was preparing for the anniversary was eaten not only by those who remembered the march, but by the mourners who remembered Georgia Gilmore.

In Martha Hawkin's book *Finding Martha's Place: My Journey Through Sin, Salvation and Lots of Soul Food,* she described her meeting with Georgia Gilmore and how Gilmore told her how to make Gilmore's famous iced tea, "the kind that Martin Luther King used to ask for seconds on."

Georgia Gilmore's Iced Tea, as told to Martha Hawkins

"The secret's all in the boiling. You boil sugar and water together first, the day before you want to serve it, then you put the tea bags in a pitcher with aluminum foil on top. The next day, you take the tea bags out, add water and just drink 'til you're tired. You can't have just one glass, you know. You will never want to stop drinking tea."[69]

2 cups cold water
3 family-size tea bags
1 cup sugar
Lemon juice to taste

Place the two cups of water in a pot and add teabags. Bring to a boil. Remove from heat. Let it sit. Pour warm tea into an empty pitcher. Add the sugar. Stir 'til sugar is dissolved. Let it sit overnight in refrigerator.

THE GREEN LANTERN

The Green family built the Green Lantern restaurant outside of the Montgomery city limits in 1933. Owner Hal Green took a big chance starting a business during the Great Depression. At first, the Green Lantern was a WOCO PEP gas station and later became a restaurant. The family owned a large, handsome hanging lantern and, after placing it at the front of the restaurant, named the restaurant after it. At the time of the Green Lantern's popularity, the location, at the intersection of McGehee and Carter Hill Roads, was considered to be outside of town.

The restaurant's rustic interior reinforced the feeling of escaping from the city and relaxing for an evening while enjoying a great meal. A collection of glass moons—a full moon and three crescents—was imbedded in the floor. They were lighted, and some sources say they blinked. The Montgomery County Historical Society has preserved the full moon. One of the many popular items served by the Green Lantern was their special cheese biscuit. The biscuits were featured when the Green Lantern hosted the first Alabama Taste Benefit of Boys' Ranches in 1974. As for the entrées on the menu, the establishment is most remembered for its steaks. The *Montgomery Independent* reminisced, "Couples favored a 'sirloin for two' that was approximately the size of a doormat." A collection of small cottages behind the restaurant was a popular destination for city dwellers who sought a respite from urban life without going on a long trip. Some sources called the cabins Montgomery's first motel.

The Green Lantern's rustic interior was a chief part of its popularity. *Courtesy of the Dot Moore Collection.*

The Green Lantern hosted the first Alabama Taste Benefit for Boys' Ranches in 1974. *Left to right*: unknown, unknown, Dorothy Moore and unknown. *Courtesy of the Dot Moore Collection.*

The cottages behind the Green Lantern restaurant offered city dwellers a respite in the country. *Courtesy of the Dot Moore Collection.*

The Green family eventually sold the restaurant to the Walton Hill Estate. In 1945, Dewey Edward Davis leased the Green Lantern Restaurant from the Walton Hill Estate for his sister-in-law, Mary Davis, to operate. Under her management, the Green Lantern became a popular steakhouse and "night spot." In addition to great food, guests enjoyed dancing and, on certain nights, bingo. In 1966, the Green Lantern moved to its present location on the Troy Highway.

The Walton Hill Estate demolished the Green Lantern in 1965 and built a branch bank that was called the Green Lantern Branch of the Union Bank and Trust. However, the old lantern out front was saved and hangs in the pylon beside the bank bulding, now a Regions Bank, to this day.

Green Lantern Bleu Cheese Dressing
(Mary Ellenberg's recipe, compliments of Paul Savalis)

I pound blue cheese, crumbled
½ cup apple cider vinegar
I quart buttermilk
I tablespoon Garlic powder
I ½ teaspoons paprika
½ cup corn oil
¼ cup catsup
Salt and pepper to taste
Combine all ingredients and refrigerate

HAMBURGER KING

Hamburgers Made to Order ALL DAY

Hunter Harrison happily slapped hamburgers on a sizzling grill and talked about how the Hamburger King got started. Actually, it is a love story—and not just for the love of hamburgers! In 1975, Hunter's father, Pat Harrison, was attending pre-med classes at Auburn University in Montgomery, and his mother, Gay Harrison, was in nursing school at Auburn University in Montgomery; they met in microbiology class. Pat Harrison was working at the Hamburger King on South Perry Street to cover his living expenses. Gay started working there to "help Pat out."[70] Near the end of their course of studies, Pat and Gay discovered that they had to attend their next level of education at different schools—which meant a long separation. They decided to discontinue their education and invest in the restaurant. They were married in 1977.

People have fond memories of the Hamburger King at South Perry Street and of Pat and Gay: "I like to stand at the counter and watch Pat and Gay. These guys have it down—Pat cooks while Gay juggles to-go orders, dining room orders and the folks at the walk-up window. Now, that's entertainment." On May 4, 1989, the *Montgomery Advertiser*'s column "South Flavor" described the Hamburger King on South Perry:

It's the smell that gets you—that unmistakable aroma of the burgers cooking on a grill. No matter how hard they try, most burger lovers can't make it past Hamburger King on South Perry in downtown Montgomery without going in for a taste. And once they've been in once—they usually come back a second time, and a third, and a fourth and a fifth.

A *USA Today* article listed Hamburger King as one of the top burger places in Alabama. Hunter told the story of when Pat was working hard and really did not comprehend the wide-reaching promotional significance of the *USA Today* article on Hamburger King. Early one afternoon, after the article had been out, the telephone rang in the restaurant. A voice on the other end of the line asked, "Is this where you get the world-famous hamburgers?" Pat hesitated a moment, and then replied, "Sure! What do you want?"[71] Such notoriety made a few more people aware of Hamburger King, but as one customer put it: "All you really need to know are that the hamburgers are damned good!"

In 1995, the Hamburger King building on South Perry was demolished so that the land could be used as a parking lot for the nearby law firm of Capell, Howard, Knabe and Cobbs. A *Montgomery Advertiser* article related that, on the day the building was to be demolished, some of the employees of the law firm were inspired to be part of the process. A reporter for the newspaper received a call that people were throwing bricks through the windows of the Hamburger King building! The caller was unaware that the lawyers who owned the building were the vandals. When the journalist showed up, the employees of the legal firm abashedly admitted to their folly—it was all in good fun.

Prior to the demolishment of its first building, Hamburger King had already moved to its 547 South Decatur Street location. By all accounts, that is where the real fun was—and has been for over twenty years. It remains a family-owned and -operated business. Pat died in 2010, and Gay has retired but has fond memories of the time that she and Pat ran Hamburger King: "We were soulmates. It was a wonderful way to live. It's a phenomenon—feels like our customers are family. We now have customers who are grandchildren of our first customers."[72] Their legacy continues, as their son, Hunter, and his wife, Angela, fry the hamburgers on the griddle, take the orders, bring food to the table and fill the take-out orders. What the menu lacks in variety, it makes up for in satisfying, burger-fueled happiness. The menu board behind the counter offers burgers, chips and drinks. Ordering a hamburger with "the works" includes mayo, ketchup,

Left: Hunter and Angela Harrison look happy while keeping customers happy. *Author's collection.*

Right: Hunter's father, Pat Harrison, started the business with his wife, Gay. *Courtesy of the Harrison family collection.*

onions, pickles and cheese. Regulars know that, after lunch, they can try a cold snicker bar or a honey bun for dessert. The consensus is "You can't beat it."

The dining room is a "no frills place" that others have described as a "hole-in-the-wall building." One fan wrote a letter to *USA Today*: "Made the old-fashioned way with grease—a hole in the wall, with stools so close to the counter you bump your knees. No vent for the smoke to clear out—real ambiance." Journalist Kelly Betts explained in the *Montgomery Advertiser*, "Every town has special places to eat, known only to long-time residents—Hamburger King is one of Montgomery's special places.…The smell of food cooking on the griddle is intoxicating, your clothes will also be intoxicating for the rest of the day. So, you may want to save it for informal days." Journalist Robyn Bradley, writing for the *Montgomery Advertiser*, noted, "Montgomery's not really known for a particular food (like Chicago pizza; New York bagels; New Orleans beignets), but if you hear people from the office say they are headed to Hamburger King—by all means, tag along."

Everyone agrees that the service at Hamburger King is as great as the burgers. Bradley wrote that the folks at Hamburger King "always have a smile on their face and greet the customers and have good service. It's always fun in there." A Facebook review declared: "Hamburger King will not disappoint! The staff will have you smiling before you leave." Another review from www.tripadvisor.com echoes that opinion: "Nothing fancy, just excellent ingredients and perfect preparation." In addition to the restaurant's simplicity and fun, Hunter said that an important part of Hamburger King's great taste is, "Everything we use is fresh." Hamburger King's food source is Alabama products—vegetables from the farmers' market and meat and dairy out of Birmingham. Hunter is confident of the food he serves, and the restaurant's motto reflects that: "If we don't eat it ourselves, we don't sell it."

In addition to the *USA Today* article, Hamburger King has received *Readers' Choice* awards since 1989—for over twenty years. In 2015, Hunter decided to compete in the World Food Championship; Hamburger King won the inaugural Montgomery Burger Bash and went on to compete in the World Food Championship in Kissimmee, Florida, where it finished at number eighteen out of thirty-nine competitors in the burger competitions.

Hunter explained his confidence in his burgers: "If the judges at the World Food Championship were anything like the voting customers in Montgomery, the reason for Hamburger King's success was a reliance on simplicity."[73] Since that competition, Hunter says, "If there's a contest list, we try to be on it."[74] In addition to the *USA Today* and *Readers' Choice* recognitions, Hamburger King has also received the 2015 aol.com Best Hamburger in the State award, and the October 18, 2001 issue of *EATS* declared Hamburger King "One of the good spots in Montgomery."

The Hamburger King painting on the side of the Hamburger King restaurant. *Author's Collection.*

Hunter, Angela and their helpers serve up about one hundred burgers a day, with smiles and greetings as customers walk through the door. Gay is proud that every governor of Alabama has eaten at Hamburger King, but she says what makes her the proudest is that all kinds of folks are comfortable and happy at Hamburger King. "A doctor will sit at the bar next to a plumber. Our customers are from all walks of life. Everybody is equal."[75] Hamburger King customers leave happy, as reviews show. "The King has made our stomachs

Tom Connor's popular *Montgomery Advertiser* column "Remember When" featured his sketches. *Courtesy of the Landmarks Foundation.*

happy with his homemade deluxe burger for lunch today." "Lawd have mercy, it sho am good!"

HILDA'S PLACE

In his popular *Montgomery Advertiser* column, "Remember When," Tom Connor called Hilda's one of Montgomery's "swankiest supper clubs." Founded in 1941, Hilda's was operated by Hilda Reynolds and located on Madison Avenue, across from the Parkmore Drive-In. The establishment is described as "a big city club with an orchestra and Montgomery's only first-rate entertainment and floor show, plus superb food." Hilda's catered to affluent Montgomery residents and top-ranking officers at the nearby Maxwell Air Force Base. Proprietor Hilda Reynolds later became Mrs. Elgin Smilie and sold the business. The establishment later became the Greek Country Club.

JUBILEE SEAFOOD RESTAURANT

You're Among Friends at Jubilee Seafood

Jubilee Seafood Restaurant is located at 1057 Woodley Road and is considered a part of the historic Cloverdale neighborhood. Cloverdale was founded in the early 1900s, when the area was known as Graham's Woods. The woods were predominately composed of pine trees, so the area was also known as the Pines. According to local lore, at times, the woods would give way to open meadows that were full of clover. As the woods were cut down to make way for fashionable Tudor and bungalow-style homes, the fields of clover inspired the development's name. Cloverdale became part of the city of Montgomery in 1928.

Jubilee Seafood has been serving Montgomery for twenty-five years. Owner and chef Bud Skinner ensures that he serves the highest quality of seafood by cutting every piece of fish that comes through Jubilee himself.

Jubilee waitress Denise Odum enjoyed her job as much as the guests enjoyed the Jubilee Seafood Restaurant. *Courtesy of the* Montgomery Advertiser.

Sous chef Josh McBride "handcrafts each dish into the perfect melody," and Scott Alexander has "stood behind Jubilee's bar for over twenty years."[76] The restaurant's website states that, at Jubilee, "quick quality service meets superior cuisine."[77] Jubilee Seafood has been featured in *USA Today* and has been acknowledged by the *New York Times*. In addition to regular dining areas, the facility offers party spaces and catering services. The website promises: "No reservation, but there is no rush—you are among friends at Jubilee Seafood."[78]

The menu offers appetizers that include a West Indies salad, sautéed and fried crab claws and baked oysters. Jubilee's dinner entrées include blackened, Greek and fried Snapper; Greek, barbequed and fried shrimp; and fried oysters. The dessert menu begins with Jubilee's popular white chocolate bread pudding, but it also includes dark chocolate and vanilla bean cheesecake and a homemade Key Lime pie.

There is a regular menu, but Skinner also prides himself on the fresh fish that he receives daily and crafts into entrées:

> *You will never get bored, because the extensive specials menu changes daily. We get fresh fish daily and offer dishes you will only find at Jubilee! Our kitchen artistically creates every plate. Grab a seat and enjoy a meal complete with your favorite brew or cocktail crafted by none other than Montgomery's best bartender, Scott. Don't forget to save room for our famous bread pudding!*[79]

Tom Connor's popular *Montgomery Advertiser* column "Remember When" featured his sketches. *Courtesy of the Landmarks Foundation.*

THE KOTTAGE

Eat Well with Bill Cordell

In 1946, Ed Bourne opened the Kottage on Mount Meigs Road. Bill Cordell was the chef, and in 1949, he bought out Bourne. In addition to being a chef, Cordell also had some talent in marketing. He created the slogan, "Eat well with Bill Cordell," and Montgomery's fried chicken lovers took him up on his offer. At the time, eating out was not yet a common a pastime, and Cordell said that part of his success was due to him "helping educate the palates of tens of thousands to 'bought out' fried chicken." Cordell later opened restaurants in other locations and enjoyed a successful thirty-year career.

MAJESTIC CAFÉ AND ROOFTOP GARDEN RESTAURANT

The Majestic Café was located on the ground floor of the Ben Moore Hotel, and the Roof Garden Restaurant was on the hotel's covered roof. D.C. "Doc" Moore built the twenty-eight-room hotel in 1945 and named it after his father, Ben F. Moore. Ben Moore was born a slave in 1848 and died in 1914, at the height of Jim Crow. The Ben Moore Hotel was built at the corner of Jackson and High Streets by Brewer Building service. Matthew Franklin Moore rented the building and opened the hotel and café on September 23, 1951. The hotel was considered to be fireproof, as it was built of brick and concrete, with block joists and window sash casings that were constructed of steel. The building's doors had solid cores and were made to resist fire for up to one hour. The Ben Moore Hotel faces High Street and has a thirty-three-foot front, and it extends along Jackson Street for one hundred feet. The hotel was the proud centerpiece of Centennial Hill, Montgomery's African American neighborhood. Centennial Hill was founded soon after the Civil War, during Reconstruction, by freedmen. The Swayne Primary School was opened in 1867 by the American Missionary Association and the Freedman's Bureau. The First Congregational Church was founded in 1872. The neighborhood took its name from the nation's founding celebrations in 1876.

At the time of the Majestic Café's opening, Montgomery's hotels were segregated; the Ben Moore was the first high-rise building constructed outside of the downtown area, and it was the first hotel in Montgomery to serve the black community. The hotel was listed in *The Negro Motorist Green Book*, which was written by Victor Hugo Green. *The Green Book*, as it was commonly called, was a list of hotels, motels, restaurants, service stations and even barber shops and beauty parlors where African Americans were legally allowed in the mid-twentieth century in the United States. The Malden Brothers Barbershop on the ground floor of the Ben Moore Hotel was also listed in *The Green Book*. The hotel did allow white guests.

According to local historian Wilhelmina Howard Harris, "The hotel earned its place in history during the early days of the civil rights movement as activists began to challenge segregationist laws in everything from transportation to dining facilities."[80] The Roof Garden Restaurant was a popular site during the 1950s and 1960s, and it played a major role during the Montgomery Bus Boycott. Black and white officials met to discuss the boycott and the "treatment blacks were receiving."[81] Dr. Martin Luther King, Dr. Ralph Abernathy and E.D. Nixon (president of the NAAPCP and the Montgomery Progressive Democratic Association) held meetings at the Roof Garden Restaurant. The rooftop location allowed the leaders of the Montgomery Improvement Association to protect themselves, as the elevation allowed them to see the surrounding streets, thus they were kept aware of any gathering mobs. Another protective structural feature of the hotel was a secret, underground room that could only be accessed through the pantry.

Above: The Ben Moore Hotel was Montgomery's first hotel to serve the African American community. The Majestic Café was a popular spot for negotiations during the Montgomery Bus Boycott. *Courtesy of the* Montgomery Advertiser.

Right: Matthew Moore opened the Ben Moore Hotel and the Majestic Café. *Courtesy of the* Montgomery Advertiser.

In her autobiography, restaurateur and public speaker Martha Hawkins remembered that her father took her family to meetings of the Montgomery Improvement Association at the Majestic Café. The Montgomery Improvement Association was organized by Montgomery ministers and leaders on December 5, 1955, after Rosa Parks refused to give up her seat to a white man on December 1, 1955. After a day-long boycott of the buses was successful, the Montgomery Improvement Association decided to continue the boycott until the City of Montgomery made some changes to their segregationist polices of the city bus system. The bus boycott continued for 382 days, although it created hardships for the African American community and reduced income for the city. Martha Hawkins's father, Willie Hawkins, told her, "It was good for us to attend. We was all learning to be free."[82]

Years later, the rooftop restaurant became a nightclub called the Afro Club. Many famous African American performers appeared there, including Tina Turner, Clarence Carter and B.B. King. After their performances, they would stay at the hotel. Ellen Sloan, the daughter of Matthew Moore and the granddaughter of the Ben Moore's namesake, sold the hotel in 1979 to Edward Davis Sr., and Edward Davis Sr. left the property to his son. The dilapidated hotel building and the Roof Garden Restaurant still stand. The Majestic Café sits like a time capsule; the carpet, chairs and tables are still in place. Since the hotel is an important landmark for civil rights and the city of Montgomery, many hope that it will be restored and repurposed.

MARTHA'S PLACE

Martha Ann Hawkins, a native of Montgomery County, dreamed of opening a restaurant when she was twelve years old. In addition to her own dreams, Martha said that she was inspired to own a restaurant by Georgia Gilmore. Gilmore is known for her active role in the civil rights movement during the Montgomery Bus Boycott; she served food in her home that became a favorite meeting place for civil rights leaders. Georgia Gilmore served such notable figures as Martin Luther King Jr. and Robert Kennedy. Gilmore also sold food to raise money for the Montgomery Bus Boycott. Martha wrote about her dream of opening a restaurant and her hard times in a memoir cookbook that was published in 2010. One reviewer of *Finding Martha's Place: My Journey Through Sin, Salvation and Lots of Soul Food* wrote that, in the book, Martha "served up the story of her journey in her homespun vernacular,

Martha's first location was in an older home on 456 Sayre Street. *Courtesy of Martha's Collection.*

along with some mouthwatering recipes." Martha described her dream in her book: "I always wanted to own my own restaurant. And not no ordinary restaurant neither. I wanted to own a special restaurant where folks can eat good food and talk about the things that matter and sort through life and feel good afterward."[83]

In October 1988, Martha made her dream come true when she opened Martha's Place at 456 Sayre Street in an old house close to downtown Montgomery. When she first walked into the house, she realized that it needed major renovations; she wrote in *Finding Martha's Place*, "No Holy Spirit was sparkling on the floorboards."[84] Getting the house in shape to become her dream restaurant took work, time and faith. When she totaled up the amount of money she needed to turn the house into her dream restaurant, "the bottom line flared up like a grease fire with no salt on hand to put it out!"[85]

She moved out of her apartment to save money and lived in the house without heat or air conditioning. She also catered events and prepared private dinners to raise money. Since her sign was out in front of the house, a lot of people in the community knew that she was working hard to make her dream come true. Finally, Martha was able to secure a bank loan to renovate and turn the house into a restaurant that sat 125 guests and featured southern-style cooking. She recorded the moment that she went and bought the licenses she needed to open her restaurant: "I signed the papers and paid my fee, and then—no joke—the people at city hall all started clapping. They stood up behind their desks and smiled and waved and cheered like I had been hired as chef of the Bellagio Hotel."[86]

Martha's restaurant was a big success. Martha was happy and proud to welcome all of her guests, but in her book, she mentioned several who were well-known:

> *In the weeks to follow, one of my first customers was a woman with large dark-rimmed glasses and a red scarf tied around her neck. She was carrying a book about Nelson Mandala, and when she sat at a table and ordered fried chicken with chitlins, I had to hold myself back from hugging her outright. "This is mighty good food," she said after she had eaten, and then motioned me closer so she could speak into my ear. "This is the food that will sustain you," she said and gave my hand a little squeeze. She promised she'd be back soon, and promised she'd be bringing her friends next time. Then she took corn bread muffins to go, she did. From that day forward, anytime she came to my restaurant, Rosa Parks always took corn bread muffins to go.[87]*

Martha's Place was also proud to host CNN when they hosted the ceremonies for the fortieth anniversary of the Montgomery Bus Boycott.

Martha's Place has since moved and is currently located at 7798 Atlanta Highway. Although many miss the ambiance of the old house on Sayre Street, the new restaurant has three large dining rooms with large windows. The kitchen is big enough to let the cooks and servers keep the food hot and tasty on the buffet serving line. Martha still starts her business day the way she did when she was in the house:

> *I gather whoever's on shift in the kitchen with me, and we all hold hands and we look upward. That's what this restaurant is built on 'cause that's all we know to do. We pray out loud, all the same time, no shushing or*

uppitiness when we talk to the good Lord. If another person's praying, then the rest of us are pursing our lips and saying "mmm," "amen" and "thank, you, Jesus" and "Yes, Lord let it be so." Every morning, that's how it goes.[88]

Martha's personality and her life story of overcoming many struggles are as famous as her restaurant. Today, she speaks to many groups and inspires them with her personal story of pursuing her dream and supporting herself without government assistance. At one point in her life, Martha attempted suicide and spent time recovering in a mental hospital. She credits her recovery and her success to her faith. She believes that her faith in God's love and mercy inspired her thinking and changed her life.

Toward the front of Martha's Place, there is a small bookcase that holds some of the awards that have recognized Martha's work. Martha was awarded the Small Business of the Year Award from the Montgomery Chamber of Commerce in 1998. In 1999, she was honored with the Eli Lilly Lifetime Foundation Achievement Award, and in that same year, she was featured in *Guidepost Magazine* for the "Best Stories of Guidepost." In 2002 and 2003, Martha was awarded the Business Legacy Award from Leadership Alabama. In 2004, she was recognized with the Ruth Fertel Keeper of the Flame Award in acknowledgement of not only Martha's business success, but the contribution of her organization, Martha Hawkins' Ministries, which helps single parents and low-income children. Martha talks about her success by talking about food:

When I think of success, I like to think of lima beans....Most lima beans are not worth the heap of dirt they was growed in. But lima beans are on my menu for a reason. The lima beans at Martha's Place are cooked with a whole lot of love. When you put them against your lips, they feel plump like you was smooching the back of your baby grandson's knee. The beans are soft and piping hot, warm, straight out of the pot they was cooked in. And if you close your eyes and let them, those lima beans will remind you of sitting at home with all the people you love, and on the supper table in front of you is spread a country banquet on a red-checked cloth, and all your friends are enjoying themselves and diving in and [helping] themselves and joking together and having a good ole time. Those lima beans are on my menu because I know how food can become more than just food. It's what a body uses for change. You take something as poor and lonely as a lima bean—on one hand, its ugly and stupid and forlorn and forgotten. But then you cook it just so, and a powerful change happens. Lima beans become something luscious—the food of delight and flavor and faith. That's why they are on the menu at Martha's Place. That's the poetry of this restaurant's life, my life, my success, this food that smacks of hope.[89]

Martha's accolades continued in 2014, when she was recognized as the Alabama State Small Business of the Year. In 2016, the Montgomery Chamber of Commerce awarded her the Point of Light Award for her outstanding business achievements and contributions to community. The River Region Ethics Small Business Award also recognized Martha in 2017.

Martha's Place offers a buffet of classic southern dishes that change with the day of the week. Some dishes include fried and baked chicken, collards, fried okra, black-eyed peas and banana and corn pudding. Martha is proud of her fried chicken: "Ain't no ordinary fried chicken neither. It's hot and juicy on the inside, with tender, crisp outsides, and it ain't never greasy. When you eat a piece of my fried chicken, you can snap your fingers afterward."[90] In her book, Martha talks a lot about the food she loves to fix: "On the menu

Martha's current location is on Atlanta Highway. *Courtesy of Martha's Collection.*

that day was steak and gravy, fried chicken, pork chop casserole, chicken and dumplings, baked ham, collards, chitlins, black-eyed peas, fried green tomatoes, sweet potato pie, peach cobbler, strawberry pie and, yes, pound cake—all the comfort food that people love."[91]

Martha's peaceful and graceful demeanor adds to the wonderful taste and texture of Martha's Place's food. Martha is known for hiring people who are "down on their luck." In her book, she states, "I developed a habit of bringing home strays whenever I found some fall from the nest."[92] She laughed when she remembered that she had once prayed, "Lord, send me your worst cases." Then, she laughed and said, "I didn't know what I was asking for!" She then changed her prayer to say, "Lord, send me those who need help who can also help me."[93] She inspires others by asking them to believe that "keeping the faith makes the difference between failure and success."[94]

Martha ended her book with a prayer of blessing "for anybody who's reading this book."[95] Then, she finishes with an invitation: "By the way, the food is always available, always piping hot, always comforting, always tasting good all the time. Y'all come on down if you're ever in Montgomery. Let Martha fix you up some real good soul food. It's mighty tasty, so y'all come now and eat up, y'hear?"[96] Anyone who loves good food knows to accept!

Sallie Hawkins's Corn Bread

1 ½ cups self-rising corn meal
½ cup self-rising flour
¼ sugar
2 eggs
2 tablespoons mayonnaise
1 cup buttermilk
4 tablespoons shortening, melted
½ cup water

Preheat the oven to 425 degrees Fahrenheit. Combine all the ingredients in a medium mixing bowl. Stir with a wooden spoon thoroughly until blended. Pour the mixture into a well-greased skillet and bake for thirty-five minutes until golden brown. Serves twelve.

MARTIN'S RESTAURANT

Home Style Cooking Since 1930

Martin's was first opened in 1930 in a small, white frame building on the corner of Carter Hill Road and Pine Leaf Street. Alice Martin, who owned the property, operated the restaurant, where she offered sandwiches and pies, for nine years. In 1939, she rented the building to David "Smitty" Smith. According to Tom Connor in his popular *Montgomery Advertiser* column "Remember When," Smitty operated the restaurant on a month-to-month basis and paid Alice Martin $32.50 in monthly rent. Martin's menu contains a history section that says David Smith also borrowed $100 from Dr. Farris Martin to take over the restaurant. Smith always said, "I kept the Martin name because of Dr. Ferris Martin, who lent me the $100 to go into business." On his first day, he started with only 19¢ in the cash register. He had already spent $32.50 on rent and had spent the rest on food, ice and other items that he needed to open. Smitty expanded the menu to include a "meat and three plate for 35¢."

The restaurant was successful and remained in business on the original site for twenty-five years. However, in 1965, it was moved to the Country Club Shopping Center, where the Winn-Dixie grocery store now stands; in 1990, it was moved to its current location at 1796 Carter Hill Road. Martin's is still in the same shopping center, but it now sits in the back, near the junction of Carter Hill and Narrow Lane Roads. Martin's is currently owned and operated by David Smith's daughter, Mary Anne Merritt. But if

A group of happy customers leave Martin's after lunch. *Author's collection.*

Martin's first location was on Pine Leaf Street. *Courtesy of Martin's Collection.*

you call Mary Anne "Mrs. Martin," she will answer to it: "I'll answer to just about anything," she laughed.[97]

Martin's menu offers a list of entrées that change with the day of the week. For example, on Monday, guests can choose from baked turkey with dressing, baked meatloaf with tomato sauce and a fried catfish filet. Looking ahead to Tuesday, the menu offers roast beef with gravy, baked barbeque pork ribs with sauce and fried chicken livers. Martin's desserts are homemade and include the popular butterscotch meringue pie and the chocolate, coconut and lemon meringue pies (the gorgeous meringue is three inches tall). Aside from the meringue pies, guests can enjoy apple, pecan and sweet potato pies. Of course, "Martin's Famous Fried Chicken" is served every day. The restaurant's side orders also vary with the weekday; some examples are stewed squash, lima beans, mashed potatoes with gravy, and pickled beets.

Haley Laurence and Jared Boyd wrote on their blog about Martin's. They stated that they were on a quest to find "Alabama's Best Meat-and-Three."[98] They had a lot of compliments for Martin's. They loved the fried chicken: "I can't imagine it getting much better than this. Fried perfectly, and there's not a bit of grease on it. There's a slight peppery note that gives it a kick."[99] They noted that guests have the option to have either a breast and a leg or the pulley bones. Owner Mary Anne Merritt said, "Everyone wants the pulley bones, but there are only so many!"[100]

Mary Anne Merritt is quick to credit long-time, loyal employees. Cook Gussie Ashley, known to all as "Miss Gussie," started working at Martin's when she was fourteen years old; she is recently retired, after working at Martin's for fifty years. Robert Benson bussed tables for over thirty years. Annie Calhoun, the floor manager, and Barbara Jackson, the cook, have both worked at Martin's for over thirty years.

Merritt said that she has been working long enough that, now, long-time customers' grandchildren have become customers. She appreciates all her guests: "I owe a big 'thank you' to all of our customers and their many years of continued support. You can cook all the food you want, but if you don't have customers and don't make them happy, you won't have a restaurant long."[101] Martin's has garnered press in *Garden and Gun* magazine and regularly wins the *Readers' Choice* award for Best Fried Chicken and Best Meat and Three. Martin's continues to be popular, and rightfully declares that it has served "home-style cooking since 1930."

MORRISON'S CAFETERIA

A Cafeteria to Meet the Demands of the People

The first Morrison's Cafeteria in Alabama was opened in Mobile in 1920. Toward the end of the decade, another location was opened in Montgomery on Commerce Street in an empty theater building. *Montgomery Advertiser* announcements stated the "old" Colonial Theatre was transformed into "a toughly up-to-date cafeteria." The cafeteria's green tile front and the repurposing of the theater-style marquee made the restaurant stand out among the other downtown buildings.

In an interview in the *Montgomery Advertiser*, the cafeteria's owner, J.A. Morrison, stated the aim of the cafeteria was to "furnish the best of food at moderate prices." An advertisement that was released for the cafeteria's opening also declared that "this is to be a cafeteria conducted upon the principle of service for the entire family." Morrison's also believed in another philosophy that may sound familiar in the current era: "Managed by Montgomery People—Montgomery Help Employed—Supplies Bought in Montgomery." No out-sourcing! R.C. Mercer was in charge of the

The downtown Morrison's Cafeteria was notable for its blue tile façade. *Courtesy of the Landmarks Foundation.*

The second Morrison's Cafeteria was located Downtown. *Courtesy of the* Montgomery Advertiser.

Montgomery Morrison's, and Mrs. Herbert Goldthwaite was the assistant manager and in charge of the dining room. In another peek into the future, the advertisement claimed, "We can prove to you that it is less expensive for you and your family to eat at Morrison's than to purchase your food from the retailer, not considering the time and expense of cooking."

The cafeteria's interior was luxurious, with giant chandeliers, carpet and white tablecloths and napkins. A double-curved staircase led to the balcony, where diners could watch guests enjoying dinner on the first floor. According to owner J.A. Morrison, the upstairs balcony was also purposely designed to be "a ladies assembly room, to be used for meetings by women's clubs." Although the interior was lavish, the menu's items were affordable. Dinner could cost as little as one dollar, and a breakfast of eggs, bacon, grits and toast cost just seven cents. These prices made the establishment popular during the Great Depression and World War II.

In 1955, the cafeteria was moved to a larger building on Lee Street. In 1970, along with many other businesses of the era, Morrison's Cafeteria opened a second restaurant in the Montgomery Mall, and a third location was opened at the Eastdale Mall. In 1983, the downtown location closed.

NAPOLI RESTAURANT

Italian Foods as Only Italians Can Prepare

Napoli Restaurant was opened in 1955 on 2351 Federal Drive, across from Gunter Field, the military base. Owner and chef Paesano Corsino advertised that he supervised all orders personally. With an Italian name and an Italian chef and owner, guests could certainly expect the menu to offer Italian food, but Napoli's also offered American dishes, such as choice charcoal steaks, fried chicken, fresh seafood sandwiches and even some Chinese dishes. Pizza was Napoli's specialty and was described as being "made fresh daily, in the authentic Italian way. No ready-prepared or frozen ingredients ever used. Try it in our dining room or for take-out orders." The restaurant's dessert offerings included "Montgomery's only spumoni ice cream."

Paesano Corsino had been a chef and proprietor at other restaurants in Montgomery before opening Napoli. He was a native of Castlelett Cervo, Italy, and immigrated to the United States on June 13, 1914. He received his citizenship papers on September 4, 1942. He received a lot

A *Montgomery City Directory* advertisement for Napoli Restaurant stated that the restaurant offered both dining-room and take-out service. *Courtesy of the Landmarks Foundation.*

of attention wherever he worked; an article in the April 24, 1938 edition of the *Montgomery Advertiser*, he announced that he was "back with [his] old friends the Franco Brothers" at the corner of Church and Lee Streets. A May 3, 1946 advertisement in the *Montgomery Advertiser* announced the grand opening of the Plaza.

Napoli's noted personnel included Chef Paesano and his nephew, Lindo Corsino. Chef Paesano promised his guests that "all dishes [were] prepared under the personal direction of Chef Paesano, famous for his European and American dishes for many years in Montgomery." On June 8, 1948, the *Montgomery Advertiser* announced that partners and owners Paesano Corsino and Nace Alhadeff were opening a new restaurant called the Roma Café at the corner of Bibb and Coosa Streets. Both men had worked together before. The article explained to the public: "Here is the place in Montgomery where you can get that real Italian spaghetti and juicy western steaks made famous by Paesano, formerly of the Plaza Night Club." Paesano Corsino also worked with Toofie Deep when the Sahara restaurant opened in 1952.

Chef Paesano later brought his sons into his business. The *Montgomery Advertiser*'s press release read that Donald Corsino, all round chef, was trained by his father, Paesano, "the old Maestro himself." Randall Corsino became an expert in spaghetti sauce and filled the position of lasagna chef. The promotion stated that Paesano Corsino was "Montgomery's only Italian chef—test and tell the difference."

The staff at Napoli celebrated the restaurant's first anniversary on September 21, 1956. The celebration's promotion headlined, "pizza pie is our specialty" and promised "free cigars and flowers" for guests who came to join in the first-year celebration. A note on the promotion stated: "We are grateful to all of our friends, customers and military personnel who made our first year a tremendous success." Napoli continued serving popular Italian and American food until 1966. Donald Corsino continued the family tradition of operating Montgomery's classic restaurants when he opened Corsino's.

PARKMORE DRIVE-IN

The South's Most Talked About Drive-In Restaurant

In the 1950s in Montgomery, Alabama—much as it was in other American cities—drive-in restaurants were gathering spots for young people. Writer Barbara Boswell described the typical drive-in:

> [It was] *the center of all that was holy to a teenager, an asphalt Mecca where young people met to swap stories about fading romances, rock-and-roll stars, the hottest girls, the coolest guys, the fastest wheels, the nastiest teachers and the squarest parents. Young people in their parents' car circled the drive-in, looking for friends, flirting and "showing off your wheels."*[102]

The Parkmore, which was owned by Ralph and Bob Williams, was perhaps the most popular of the several drive-ins in Montgomery. One of the reasons for its popularity among teenagers was its live radio show, *Parkmore Platter Time*, that was broadcast right before their eyes—and ears! Disc jockey Bob Conrad was perched in the big glass studio atop the restaurant at 3036 Mount Meigs Road, spinning records and reading dedications. The source of the dedications were teenagers who called into the disc jockey from their home telephones. They would then drive over to the Parkmore, munch on french fries and sip on cherry Cokes as they waited to hear their dedication. Another fun element of the Parkmore was that its waitresses would arrive

𝒯𝒽ℯ 𝒫arkmore
DRIVE-IN RESTAURANT
Specializing In
Chicken In The Basket — Fountain Service
Courteous Curb Service
Atlanta Highway at City Limits

Top: The Parkmore Drive-In was a teenager's dream hangout, even though this photo shows a quiet parking lot. *Courtesy of the Alabama Department of Archives and History.*

Bottom: This *Montgomery City Directory* advertisement promotes the favorite menu item, "Chicken in the Basket." *Courtesy of the Landmarks Foundation.*

on roller-skates, and an advertisement promised that they would also be courteous. Hamburgers were popular menu items at the drive-in, but so was the "chicken in a basket."

The Parkmore Drive-In's address was 2500 Mount Meigs Road, but it was later changed to 3036, when the city changed the road's numbering. Finally, that part of Mount Meigs Road was renamed Atlanta Highway. The Parkmore Drive-In was closed in the late 1960s.

PONT ROUGE

The Pont Rouge (red bridge) restaurant got its name from two elements. The first was its location on Jackson Hospital's third-story bridge over Pine Street, which connected the hospital to the physicians' building. The second element was its elegant red and gold décor. People still remember the restaurant's red furniture, red flocked wallpaper and multi-paged red menus with gold tassels—the waiters also wore red jackets.

Administrator Douglas Goode is credited with the creation of the Pont Rouge. He was inspired to establish the restaurant when he realized that there were no restaurants near the hospital, as it was in a residential area at that time. The unusual establishment hosted both the community at-large and Jackson Hospital's ambulatory patients. When their doctors approved, patients were able to join their friends and family for dinner.

Martin Lehners's ice sculptures made Sundays special. *Courtesy of the Lehners family collection.*

Martin Lehners's ice sculptures added to holiday fun. This photo shows an ice Easter bunny. *Left to Right*: Ruth Lehners, Marilyn Lehners, Diana Lehners, Jane Lehners and, in a safe carrier, their pet rabbit. *Lehners family collection.*

Pont Rouge was a popular destination from 1964 to 1983. In addition to its lush red and gold décor, Pont Rouge's guests enjoyed its open grill, where they could see their steaks being cooked over a leaping flame. Listed on the menu under "Broiler House Suggestions," the items available for the grill included char-broiled spring chicken, lamb chop, pork chop and veal cutlet. Patrons could even order a steak shish kabob that was brought to the table in flames. The menu also included fried fantail shrimp, trout almondine and fried frog legs. Sandwiches that were served with fries were also available; the options included grilled cheese, corned beef and the Pont Rouge hamburger deluxe. The dessert list was prefaced by a statement that declared, "Our pastry is hand-crafted in our own kitchen." The dessert choices included apple custard, pecan pie, ice cream, layer cake and cheesecake (a trusted source recalled that the cheesecake had a sour cream frosting). Another dessert favorite at Pont Rouge was vanilla ice cream with a crème de menthe topping. The restaurant's personable staff included Martha Eagerton, the director of dietary services; Florence Royal, a popular hostess; Chef Reuban; headwaiter Spencer Carter; server Willy Calhoon; and food manager Martin Lehners.

Food manager Martin Lehners is fondly remembered as always having a joke or a story to tell. Lehners also gained fame for his ice sculptures. Every Sunday, he would create a sculpture from a three-hundred-pound block of ice. He also constructed a box with a color wheel that would shine up through the ice. The ice sculptures and Martin Lehners's friendly personality were important parts of Pont Rouge's popularity.

Guests who were not patients at Jackson Hospital would enter through the lobby and go up to the third floor. Despite being attached to a hospital and accommodating hospital patients (who wore gowns, pajamas and robes), many guests insist that the elegant atmosphere made them feel like they were in a sophisticated and expensive New York restaurant. But no matter how sophisticated the establishment was, the prices were extremely reasonable, as the restaurant functioned on a non-profit basis. Pont Rouge was closed in the early 1980s.

POP MYERS POPCORN

By My Corn, I Shall Be Known

Pop Myers Popcorn operated a popular popcorn and drink stands in two locations. One stood on Forest Avenue, near Oak Park, where a yummy box of hot popcorn and a cool drink were welcome treats after a romp at the park. The second location was on 923 East Fairview Avenue, near Cloverdale School and the school's adjoining sports field. Students, hungry after a long day of learning, and ball players and their fans, thirsty after playing and cheering, all thronged to Pop's for cold drinks and delicious popcorn. One of Pop's most popular items, "shake ice," were partially frozen bottled Cokes that were named shake ice because they were "chilled just to the point, where, if you'd shake 'em, they would turn to ice just as you opened them."[103] Pop's was also known for freezing chocolate candy bars, including Milky Ways and Hershey bars. Some parents had an

Pop Meyers's Popcorn stand in Old Cloverdale was popular with adults and kids alike. *Courtesy of the Pugh Collection.*

agreement, whereby their children would get whatever treats they wanted during the week, and then the parents would stop by the stand and pay the tab at the end of the week.

Pop Myers Popcorn's story began on July 1, 1922, when Marcus Barnabus Myers (M.B. Pops) set up a business with a popcorn popper at the East gate of Oak Park. Along with his popcorn popper, he posted his slogan, "By my corn, I shall be known." His daughter Mary Louise Myers Pugh wrote, "His popcorn was a nickel and stayed a nickel until his famous stand was closed on September 1, 1952." Pugh continues to tell the family story that, during the summer months, Pop was fine outside; but when winter came, especially during rain or other bad weather, Pop would move into the Oak Park pavilion. On one cold November day, Mr. Bogacki, a friend and neighbor who lived across the street from the park, saw Pop selling popcorn in the cold and walked over to him, saying, "Pop, you can't stay out in this bad weather. I'm going to build you a stand." A few weeks later, Mr. Bogacki delivered the stand at Forest Avenue. He had designed and built it, and it was the answer to a dream. Pop's business grew by leaps and bounds after the popcorn stand was built.[104]

M.B. Myers moved his brother Jerome and his family to Montgomery in 1932 and opened another popcorn stand on East Fairview Avenue in Cloverdale. While both establishments and their proprietors were known simply as "Pops," Jerome Myers, who manned the East Fairview store, was known as Pop Jr. to Cloverdale students, the firemen at the nearby Cloverdale station and residents of Cloverdale. Marcus Barnabus Myers ran the first popcorn stand on Forest Avenue. He is remembered for his compassion and generosity when visiting the children in the nearby hospital and bringing them small gifts.

At the East Fairview Avenue location, Jerome Myers posted pictures of the kids in the neighborhood and cards on his philosophy of life inside the stand. One well-remembered postcard was from a former truckdriver who used to make deliveries down the street at the Montgomery Country Club. After he made his stops, he would go to Pop's for a snack. Pop and the truck driver became friends. The postcard was sent from the movie set of *Love Me Tender* and read, "Pop, did you ever think I'd make it this far?" It was signed "Elvis."[105]

A poster at Pop's encouraged patrons to smile and claimed that popcorn was "America's oldest and best confection." The advertisement also declared that popcorn was healthy, because it was "both a food and a ruffage." Pop's was also the only business to sell white instead of yellow popcorn. Myers' Popcorn was popular for many years at both sites, and although the advertisement requested it, no one at Pop's found it difficult to smile!

THE RANCH MOTEL DINING ROOM

Under the Sign of the Whirling Lariat

The Ranch's location, three miles south of Montgomery on U.S. Routes 31, 80, 231 and 82, was advertised as "within the city limits" and provided a fun location for family outings. The Ranch was on the "Recommended by Duncan Hines" and AAA lists. Families on vacation often sought out restaurants that were on the Duncan Hines list, as they guaranteed good food and good service. In 1930, the man who later established the Duncan Hines food company wrote and self-published a guide that included a list of 167 recommended restaurants that he titled, *Adventures in Good Eating*. Duncan Hines's guide became so popular that his recommendation became

Left: The fun menu advertised dining-room and car service. *Courtesy of the Montgomery County Historical Society.*

Below: The journey to the Ranch restaurant was a bit of a drive, but the restaurant was advertised as "within city limits." *Courtesy of the Montgomery County Historical Society.*

"a nationally recognized seal of approval." The popularity of his restaurant guides led to his later success in the food business.

The menu at the Ranch Motel was, as one may have expected, composed completely of American fare. However, as one might also expect in Montgomery, the menu offered a large selection of seafood. A graphic of a wagon train ran across the bottom of the menu, and a cowboy on a horse with a lariat dominated the cover. Inside the menu, the "Ranch Specialties" included baked roulettes of fresh flounder, baked stuffed crabs and a combination seafood platter. Other fresh seafood options included rock lobster tails, fried oysters, french-fried jumbo Gulf shrimp, broiled and fried red snapper, french-fried fresh red snapper fingers, fresh shrimp à la maison and fresh fried filet of flounder. All of the restaurant's seafood entrées were served with French fries and tartar sauce. The ranch also offered "fried Ranch chicken," which was described as "[one-half of a] young, milk-fed chicken, fried a golden brown, served with shoestring potatoes."

A list of steaks under the heading "Ranch Parade of Steaks" included a "Cowboy steak" that was a "U.S. choice sirloin strip with the bone left in to insure a juicy, delicious steak." The steak parade also included broiled Kansas City, tenderloin and filet mignon. The grilled steaks on parade were sirloin and chopped steak, and they were both served with french-fried onions. The "Special Dishes Sure to Please" included barbecued pork spareribs and a barbecued half milk-fed chicken. The restaurant's entrées also deviated from American cuisines and included the "Ranch spaghetti" (noted as "it's different"), chicken tetrazzini ("Served in a casserole." Don't let the name fool you—this is delicious) and spaghetti cacciatore ("this dish is spaghetti at its best"). The Ranch's sandwiches included ham and barbecued pork and beef. The popular hamburger, cheeseburger, and grilled cheese were also available. Other traditional favorites were the club sandwich, which was described as a "three decks deluxe," and a bacon and tomato sandwich. The restaurant's salads included a shrimp salad, a chef salad and a tomato stuffed with shrimp or chicken. Take-out service was also offered. The Ranch served guests from 7:00 a.m. to 12:00 a.m. The Ranch Motel Dining Room was officially closed in the 1970s.

THE RED BIRD INN

The Red Bird Inn was located on Seibels Road. It was opened in the 1920s and closed around 1983. An advertisement from 1957 named Floy Jamison as the owner. Comments from the Facebook page "Times Gone By" repeatedly praise the Inn's fried chicken and onion rings. One comment described the dishes as "just a little taste of heaven." Another remembered that, when returning home with take-out orders, it was "all they could do not to eat them all before they got home." On another Facebook page titled "I Ate Chicken at the Red Bird Inn," a funny story was told about a gentleman that took his date out to dinner at the Red Bird Inn. For reasons unknown, the young lady was, bewilderingly, not impressed with

The Red Bird Inn sign hung in front of the restaurant. *Courtesy of the* Montgomery Advertiser.

her dinner. The gentleman then took her home and came back to the Red Bird Inn for seconds.

The take-out menu offered chicken dinners and allowed guests to choose white meat, dark meat or mixed. Chicken livers and gizzards were also offered on the menu, along with a fried shrimp dinner. Orders came with coleslaw and the customer's choice of french-fried potatoes or potato salad. The restaurant's specialties included steaks and chicken and "your favorite beverage." Guests brought their own alcoholic beverages; one guest reminisced, "I remember my dad bringing in a bottle," and another said, "We'd bring in a cooler of beer." An advertisement noted that the private dining rooms were air-conditioned. Claiming to be "Montgomery's oldest catering service," the Red Bird Inn stated, "We cater to private parties and family groups." The Red Bird Inn was open Tuesday through Saturday, from 11:00 a.m. to 9:30 p.m.

The first Red Bird Inn's building burned. The second building was constructed from the recycled lumber of old army barracks and was a series of small rooms. Each room had booths, where curtains could be pulled for privacy. Another fun touch was the jukebox on the wall of each sitting area.

Everyone's favorite waiter was George. Part of the kitchen was visible, and people also remembered the cook, Teresa, who battered and fried chicken so fast that "flour was dusting everywhere."

THE RED BIRD INN'S FRIED CHICKEN AND ONION RING RECIPE

Mix a package of non-fat dry milk, as directed. Add salt and pepper. Store in refrigerator overnight. Remove skin from chicken. Dip chicken in milk, roll in flour, dip back in the milk, then back in the flour. Make sure grease is hot, and fry!

SAHARA RESTAURANT

Make Yourself at Home

The Sahara Restaurant at 511 East Edgemont Avenue advertised that it would hold a grand opening on December 10, 1952, at 12:00 p.m. Restaurateurs and chefs Toofie Deep and Sesto Paesano Corsino offered "choice charcoal broiled steaks, selective seafoods, famous Italian spaghetti and ravioli and other incomparable Chinese dishes." The announcement asked, "For you, your family and your friends to make the Sahara your headquarters for all festivities." The grand opening invitation read as follows: "You are cordially invited to visit our new restaurant. Everything has been carefully planned and is now in readiness to render people the finest in food preparation." The proprietors took out a full-page advertisement in the *Montgomery Advertiser*, and they later had it framed. Chef Paesano's son, Don Corsino, kept the framed advertisement on a wall in his restaurant, Corsino's, for over twenty years.

Deep explained that they named the restaurant the Sahara because, "There was nothing out here then. The streets were not paved, and Normandale did not exist." The location was close to the Cloverdale Idlewild neighborhood and, later, the Normandale Shopping Center and suburb. Cloverdale Idlewild is next to Cloverdale, one of the first suburbs in Montgomery, and was at one time a part of the Mastin family plantation. The development of the land started in the late 1920s. Also a part of the Mastin family land, Normandale's residential development coincided with the construction of the Normandale Mall in 1954. The location of the Sahara, near these neighborhoods and the main thoroughfare, increased its popularity.

According to Tom Connor, who wrote the popular *Montgomery Advertiser* column "Remember When," before the Deep family operated the Sahara Restaurant, they ran the Blue and Gray Grill on Church Street. During the Great Depression, many people were hungry; pedestrians in downtown Montgomery were often approached by strangers asking for food. Connor wrote that "Toofie Deep kept a big pot of stew on the stove all the time, and it was served just as freely and cheerfully to those who couldn't pay as to those who could."

The Sahara's menu was exciting right from the cover, which featured a sheik in flowing robes riding a camel with a pyramid in the background. One of the most popular dishes was "West Indies salad"; it was described as "[One-half] pound all white crab meat, onions, vinegar and oil." A more telling statement accompanied that description: "Through the courtesy of Bayley's Restaurant in Mobile, Alabama, we are pleased to offer you his famous 'West Indies salad.'" The Sahara's other entrées included steak,

An advertisement from the *Montgomery City Directory* lists the variety of dishes available at the Sahara Restaurant. *Courtesy of the Landmarks Foundation.*

115

Left: A fire on April 26, 1987, caused extensive damage to the Sahara Restaurant. *Courtesy of the* Montgomery Advertiser.

Below: The Sahara sign was a Montgomery landmark. *Courtesy of the* Montgomery Advertiser.

lamb, chicken, calf liver, ham steak, shrimp, red snapper and veal cutlets. The popular Sahara shrimp creole was described as "fresh-caught Gulf shrimp, prepared in the traditional Creole manner." The Sahara even offered some Chinese dishes—shrimp and chicken chow mein, chop suey plain and chicken chop suey. The Sahara was also proud of its pizza. On the back of the menu, patrons could find "The Story of Pizza": "Tourists once were advised to 'see Naples and die.' Better advice is to eat the dish that Naples gave to the world, pizza, and live. Pizza, as served by the Sahara, is Neapolitan style, with several choices of delicious toppings." The flap of the menu encouraged patrons to "just sit back and relax, enjoy yourself—that's just what we're here to help you do."

On Saturday, April 26, 1987, the Sahara suffered a damaging fire. The call to the firefighters was logged at 3:21 a.m., and the truck and other vehicles arrived two minutes later. They found the restaurant "well involved in flames." Owner Toofie Deep Jr. said that the fire was "leaping from the roof of the building" when he arrived. Deep told *Montgomery Advertiser* reporter Virginia Martin that rebuilding would start at once. He thought it might take about two months (to completely rebuild the Sahara). The kitchen was heavily damaged, and the interior was smoke damaged. Deep was worried about his employees and said he would continue to pay them throughout the rebuilding of the restaurant. The journalist noted that the Sahara was "considered one of the gathering places of the Alabama legislators while in Montgomery in session. Walls are lined with oil paintings of eight former governors." The Sahara Restaurant did rebuild and celebrated its fiftieth anniversary in 2002. However, it closed around 2005.

SINCLAIR'S

Come On Out To Sinclair's

Sinclair's was opened in 1992 at 1051 East Fairview Avenue, in the business district of the historic Cloverdale neighborhood. Cloverdale was one of the first suburbs in Montgomery and was founded in the early 1900s, largely because the extensive trolley line made living outside of the Montgomery city limits convenient. Cloverdale became a part of the city of Montgomery in 1928. The Sinclair's website describes the interior as "a friendly neighborhood bistro atmosphere."[106] Some of the restaurant's fun décor elements were the photographs of the building that were taken when it served as a service station in the 1950s. The Sinclair's website stated that "the menu was created and perfected by D.J. and Bill."[107] Sinclair's in Cloverdale closed on May 30, 2017. The Sinclair's website stated that proprietors Bill and D.J. Flippo retired and began "a new chapter in their lives."[108]

Sinclair's East was opened at 7847 Vaughn Road in November 1996 in response to the eastward movement of Montgomery's businesses and residences. The restaurant's clientele included shoppers, people meeting after work and the audience members of the Alabama Shakespeare Festival before and after shows. The Sinclair's website states that Sinclair's East "stands alone in the upscale East Montgomery area, with a casual atmosphere and excellent menu." Lunch and dinner are served Wednesday through Saturday, from 11:00 a.m. to 10:00 p.m. Brunch is served on Saturday and Sunday from 11:00 a.m. to 2:30 p.m., and the website is confident that "the weekend brunches are very special." The brunch menu includes East Fairview eggs (although the restaurant no longer has the Fairview address), eggs Benedict, eggs Soho and the signature "Crabbie Eggs," which are eggs with crab cakes. Fans of the Cloverdale location are assured that "D.J.'s she-crab soup recipe is safe and sound at Sinclair's East."[109]

The Sinclair's East lunch menu features a variety of sandwiches: beef on a bun (roast beef and provolone cheese), a shrimp sandwich

People in Cloverdale and the surrounding areas enjoyed eating dinner at Sinclair's and catching the latest movie at the Capri. *Author's collection.*

(crisp, panko-battered shrimp on a Kaiser roll) and a BLT American classic. Sinclair's chicken sandwiches include the Monterey (with bacon and Monterey cheese), pepper jack (with artichoke spread, pepper jack cheese, sautéed mushrooms and onion), Swiss (Swiss cheese and sautéed mushrooms), Hawaiian (marinated and served with ham, grilled pineapple and Monterey Jack cheese) and Cajun (blackened and served with pepper jack cheese, sautéed peppers and onions). The restaurant's burger platters are popular and served with a Kosher spear, lettuce, tomato and a choice of fries or onion rings. Some of the burgers are the backyard burger, front yard burger (with bearnaise butter and purple onion), garden burger and the well-known black and bleu burger (blackened and topped with bleu cheese crumbles). The lunch specialties are Mama Nina's spaghetti pie, made with a combination of beef and turkey; fish and chips; and pizza Delmar, which features fresh vegetables on a flour tortilla, with marina sauce and mozzarella cheese

The dinner menu also offers burger platters. Its pasta selections include vegetable Athenian, which is zucchini, mushrooms, artichoke hearts, black olives, parmesan and feta cheese sautéed and simmered in a Greek tomato sauce and served over angel hair pasta. Shrimp Athenian includes shrimp, black olives and feta cheese; another shrimp and pasta dish is a shrimp pesto. Two of the restaurant's other interesting pastas are chicken carbonara and Cajun carbonara—carbonara pastas are an Italian specialty that combine pasta with eggs, bacon and cheese. The specialties of the house include

The Sinclair's building in Cloverdale was originally a gas station. *Courtesy of the Sinclair's collection.*

stroganoff filet of tenderloin and a bleu Cajun filet. The popular Uncle Buck's shrimp is shrimp stuffed with feta cheese and herbs, wrapped in bacon and deep fried. The featured chicken dishes are honey pecan chicken, chicken piccata, Hawaiian chicken and pepper jack chicken.

While loyal customers miss the Cloverdale location of Sinclair's, there are a lot of memories to be made at the new location.

SUSIE'S DRIVE-IN

Susie's Drive-In was owned by the Smith family—James D. Smith; his two sons, J.D. and Willie; and his daughter, the drive-in's namesake, Susie. Located at 750 West Fairview Avenue, Susie's was another popular place with the teenagers; they cruised there in cars and parked just to see who else might be driving around or eating. Susie's was the drive-in of choice for the Beta Gammas from Lanier High School. Writer Ruth Ott recalled that J.D. and Willie were both members of Beta Gamma, and if a girl was dating a

Susie's Drive-In was popular, although it was located farther from a main thoroughfare than other drive-ins. *Courtesy of the Farmers Market Café collection.*

member of the fraternity, they would become a part of the scene at Susie's. Rumors and memories maintain that minors could obtain beer and other alcoholic drinks at Susie's. Sometimes, romance was in the air at Susie's. In a nostalgic online post, an entry recalled a few memories from Susie's: "All three of us girls went there on weeknights in high school. My two friends married guys they met there and are still married to them." Sadly, Susies's Drive-In is now closed.

VINTAGE YEAR

The Vintage Year restaurant is located at 405 Cloverdale Road, a part of the historic Cloverdale neighborhood. Cloverdale was established in the early 1900s. The stately tudor- and bunglow-style homes were designed by Montgomery's leading architects at the time, including Weatherly Carter, Frank Lockwood Sr. and Frank Lockwood Jr. The historic neighborhood remains one of Montgomery's most popular residential areas. Dinnner is served Tuesday through Saturday, from 5:00 p.m. to 10:00 p.m.; its popular Sunday brunch welcomes patrons from 10:30 a.m. to 2:00 p.m. The Vintage Year's building was the location of the Capistrano Club in the late 1970s. Then, in 1984, Judy and John Martin opened Montgomery's only specialty wine shop at that location. They later added gourmet lunches to complement their extensive selection of wine. They then transitioned to a white-tablecloth, fine-dining restaurant. Judy Martin was the chef, and John Martin worked the floor. That Vintage Year restaurant closed in the late 1990s.

From 2005 to 2010, the building housed the Chop House at Vintage Year, which focused on steaks. The current restaurant's manager, Bryan Trammel, noted that traces of the old Chop House lettering can still be seen in certain light on the large window in the bar area. The restaurant underwent remodeling before its current grand opening, which took place on December 15, 2015. The new owner of the Vintage Hospitality Group, Jud Blount, wanted to "bring back some of the flair it had as the original Vintage Year."[110] Although the restaurant has changed owners several times and has been remodeled and restaffed, today's Vintage Year's focus remains very similar to the original: "The Vintage Year is dedicated to providing our guests with the finest cut meat, the freshest seafood, outstanding wines and spirits, along with excellent service."[111]

The Vintage Year has dining inside and on the patio. *Author's collection.*

The Vintage Year is known for upscale dining, "featuring fine meat and seafood dishes with a Southern twist." *Forbes Magazine* reinforced the Vintage Year's history and fine-dining aspects: "[The] upscale Vintage Year Restaurant has been a local staple for a few decades."[112] The Vintage Year's menu features a variety of meats and seafood. Its starters include two dishes, oysters on the half shell and baked oysters, a nod to Montgomery's historic love for oysters. Two of the restaurant's Southern starters are fried green tomatoes and fried squash blossoms. Its main entrées include the "Catch of the Day," along with Gulf snapper and yellow-fin tuna. Lamb, prime ribeye and black angus filet are some of the offerings for serious meat-eaters.

The Vintage Year knows Montgomery, and its formal menu is proud to include "the Vintage Year burger." In fact, the Vintage Year even has a popular burger night on Tuesday; its offerings include a cowboy burger, with candied jalapenos; a Cali burger, a six-ounce turkey burger with avocado; a garden burger, a veggie mix with crème fraiche; and the newest burger twist—a blended burger with guajillo chili sorghum glaze. The Vintage Year's blended burger, which is a burger with finely chopped mushrooms, won the James Beard Blended Burger Award in August 2019.

The Vintage Year's brunch is a popular Sunday treat. Some of the restaurant's special brunch entrées include chicken and waffles, eggs Benedict with crab cakes, biscuits and gravy and, of course, shrimp and grits. Other Southern touches for brunch include collard greens and Alabama Conecuh sausage. Being in-step with tradition as well as new innovations, the Vintage Year created a series of dinners titled, "Tribute Dinners," which featured entrées from classic Montgomery restaurants that have closed. The restaurants featured were the Elite, the Sahara, the Blue Moon and the original Vintage Year. All Tribute Dinners were sellouts.

In addition to the Vintage Year, the Vintage Hospitality Group owns the Vintage Café across the street. However, Jud Blount's and Vintage Year chef Rivera's world extends well beyond restaurant and kitchen walls. The *Montgomery Advertiser* reported on the restaurant's involvement with two groups that are committed to responsible seafood consumption and fishing. The Vintage Hospitality Group joined the Share the Gulf Initiative, which is "a coalition of chefs, restaurants, seafood businesses, fishermen, conservationists and consumers who want to keep local Gulf fishing and seafood industries fair and strong." Share the Gulf was created to raise the awareness for the need of management in fishing- and seafood-related businesses in order to keep them sustainable. Vintage Year executive chef Eric Rivera and other chefs from around the Gulf met with congressional staff in Washington, D.C., to express their concerns over "key sustainability issues that directly affect the Gulf and the area's seafood."[113] Chef Rivera explained that years of mismanagement involving recreational fishing has led to unsustainable overages. Rivera believes that all groups involved can work together to each other's mutual advantage by finding a plan that "gives recreational anglers the flexibility and certainty they want and deserve while ensuring Americans can continue to enjoy red snapper and other gulf seafood now and into the future."[114] Chef Rivera further stated that the Vintage Year is "proud and grateful to have the Gulf so close…we need to protect its fishing and seafood industries."[115]

Montgomery's restaurants have historically offered seafood; Alabama residents have always loved seafood. Seafood, especially oysters, have been a food staple since the first white settlers arrived, and there is a lot of evidence that shows the importance of seafood for the native peoples. Early Spanish explorers discovered tall middens of oyster shells that testified to both the abundance and the appreciation of seafood for many seasons prior to European exploration. The mounds of shells were so numerous that white settlers used the shells as building materials and in street construction.

Award-winning Vintage Year chef Eric Rivera has plenty to smile about. *Vintage Year collection.*

Old Shell Road in Mobile, Alabama, retains the shells in its name, if not in its construction. To those who live by the Gulf, and, later, those who lived within shipping distance, there has always seemed to be a limitless supply of available seafood, from ancient times to the early contemporary era. However, the distressing modern fact is that 90 percent of the world's fisheries are either fully fished or overfished.

In addition to "Share the Gulf," the Vintage Year is a part of the James Beard's Smart Catch Program, an organization that provides training and support to chefs so that they can "serve seafood fished or farmed in environmentally responsible ways."[116] The program is detailed and nationwide. When a restaurant meets the requirements of James Beard's Smart Catch Program, it earns an emblem that it can display. This gives "consumers a simple way to identify and support restaurants" that are working with groups to keep seafood safe and available for years to come.[117]

The Vintage Year's recent awards include the Diner's Choice Award for 2019, the Wine Spectator Award of Excellence and the James Beard Foundation Featured Chef for 2019. Firmly and proudly rooted in decades-old location and tradition, the Vintage Year happily and successfully serves a modern clientele and works and plans for a sustainable future regarding food sources. The Vintage Year offers tradition and a contemporary style side by side.

Seafood Dynamite for a Dynamite Party
(seafood dip with bread, serves twenty)

2 cups rock shrimp
2 cups Gulf shrimp, diced

2 cups oysters, diced
2 cups scallops, diced
2 cups andouille sausage, diced
2 cups poblano peppers, diced
2 tablespoons garlic
2½ tablespoons kosher salt
¼ cup oil blend
2 tablespoons Masters's cajun seafood
2 tablespoons smoked paprika
3 tablespoons sweet paprika
1 teaspoon cayenne pepper
2 tablespoons coriander
6 cups aioli
2 cups crème fraiche
2 cups green onion
2 cups parmesan cheese

Start with a cold pot. Add oil, garlic and spices. Simmer over low heat. Add poblano peppers and all seafood. Simmer on low heat until seafood is just cooked. Remove from heat. Remove seafood from liquid and cool completely. Save liquid. In a large bowl, mix crème fraiche and aioli until well incorporated. Add parmesan cheese and liquid to make sauce. Fold sauce into seafood mixture. May store in refrigerator. Heat to serving temperature when ready to serve. Serve with bread.

3.
It's Greek To Me

Several of Montgomery's most beloved and classic restaurants were founded by Greek immigrants and their descendants. Today, the Greek community maintains a strong presence in Montgomery's restaurant industry. Sandra Polizos, writer and member of a Greek restaurant family, noted, "Not everyone who was Greek was a restaurant owner, but I would say the overwhelming majority were."[118] In a *Montgomery Advertiser* article, Charles Kamburis explained that "after immigrating here from the old country, they brought their cooking skills with them." However, they did not open restaurants that featured Greek food. In the same newspaper article, Sandra Moulas explained that, at the time, Montgomery "did not really have a palate that was broad enough to like different ethnic foods." Instead, Charles Kamburis explained, "They prepared what everybody was used to eating." Theo Katechis stated, "Most were meat-and-threes. They fixed what the people wanted in this area."

When a new family member arrived in the United States, many Greek families had a restaurant where the newly arrived family member could work and learn how the business was run. Charles Kamburis said that many only spoke Greek when they first arrived. Theo recalled that his father, the founder of Chris' Hot Dogs, once told him that he only went to school for six weeks. Sandra Polizos said, "They worked hard, saved their money and opened their own restaurants."[119]

Many of those restaurants became a part of Montgomery's history. Journalist Tom Connor, in his popular *Montgomery Advertiser* column "Remember When," provided a quick history of the establishments on the

Chris' Hot Dogs celebrated its one hundredth anniversary with a block party. Among the bands that entertained the crowd was the Shouting Stones. *Author's collection.*

second block of Dexter Avenue. He described the establishments as follows, "Lined up were Chris' [Hot Dogs], McGehee's, Rosemont's and Turk's. Turk's was owned by Mr. Labe Turk and was described as 'one of Montgomery's favorite meeting places.'" Connor also explained an ownership shuffle that occurred after World War II. Pete Xides, who owned the Elite Café, bought the Krystal, which was next door to him, from Ernest Pappanastos. Then, Pappanastos bought Turk's and changed the name to the Arcadia. Labe Turk then moved up on Commerce Street and opened a restaurant that became the forerunner of Gus' Restaurant, a popular breakfast and lunch spot owned by Gus Kossefis. It seemed that Greek restaurateurs were always busy keeping existing restaurants prosperous and opening new restaurants.

The following is a brief list of some of the more well-known restaurants owned by Greek proprietors:

Mr. Pappanastos operated a newstand and hot dog emporium, where, later, the Elite and Casino lounge reigned.

Pete Xides was the original owner and operator of the Elite Café and Casino Lounge and was followed by his son, Ed. The Elite Café and Casino Lounge was a Montgomery favorite from 1911 to 1990.

George Pappanastos ran the B&B Café, which later became the B&B Cafeteria in the early 1900s.

Christopher Anastasios Katechis founded Chris' Hot Dogs; Theo (Christopher Katechis' son) and Costas "Gus" (Theo's son) now run Chris' Hot Dogs. Chris' Hot Dogs is Montgomery's oldest restaurant that remains in operation; it was opened in 1917 and remains popular.

Nick Polizos, Gus Polizos and Vick Fivgas were co-owners of the Riveria Restaurant on Mobile Highway from 1955 to 1979.

Charles Z. Capanas ran the Candlelight in the 1940s.

Pete Gallis and Pete Stratas opened the Acme and Town Tavern, which operated from 1905 to the 1950s.

Tony Kamburis operated the Union Coffee Shop and the Normandy Café in the 1940s.

Mike and Sandra Miaoulis ran the Seven Seas Restaurant from late 1953 until around 1965.

Nick Polizos was a co-owner of the Azalea Manor Restaurant on Atlanta Highway. The Azalea Manor Restaurant is now closed.

George Fivgas and Sandra Moulas operated the Capitol Grill on Mount Meigs Road. When Fivgas returned to Greece, Dimitri Polizos operated the Capitol Grill, along with his sister, Magdalene Calanbakas. The Capitol Grill was closed on December 11, 2010.

State Representative Dimitri Polizos opened Mr. Gus' Ristorante (named after his father, Gus Polizos) in 2008. It is currently operated by Michael Passineau, who is assisted by Magdalene Calambakas.

All of these restaurants made for interesting family holiday planning. Most of the owners knew each other—if they were not part of an extended family. During the holidays, Sandra Polizos remembered, "It wasn't just what house we were going to, but what restaurant. All my dad's friends owned restaurants."[120]

Along with their good food, the Greek community is known for being good neighbors. They built the Greek Orthodox Church of the Annunciation on the corner of South Capitol Parkway and Mount Meigs Road; it is a significant contribution to Montgomery's historical neighborhood, Capitol Heights and to Montgomery's architectural history. Capitol Heights' development, like Cloverdale, came about when Montgomery's city trolley service made living outside of the city's limits convenient. The neighborhood was founded around 1908 and was named for its proximity to downtown and the fact that its location is 150 feet higher than the main part of the capital city. Its cozy bungalow-style homes attracted people who worked downtown but enjoyed coming home to quieter surroundings. The neighborhood has been historically described as "working class," and that certainly fits with its hard-working Greek residents.

The Greek community has also maintained a strong spiritual presence in Montgomery. The Greek Orthodox Church of the Annunciation received its charter in 1945. However, a lack of building materials delayed its construction until after World War II. The church's website explains:

> [The church] *was constructed in 1947 as the fulfillment of a dream of the small, industrious Greek community which had immigrated to Montgomery over the previous seventy years. The construction was delayed by depression and war, but the money was raised by bake sales, penny jars and poker winnings of the earliest fifteen families. Their achievement offered a place for the small Greek community to cling together, support one another and maintain their faith.*[121]

The church makes use of the many fine cooks in its congregation and offers one of Montgomery's favorite yearly events: The Labor Day Barbecue. An assortment of barbecued meats, sides and Greek desserts have been sell-out successes in the city of Montgomery for over seventy years.

The Greek immigrants came to Montgomery in search of economic opportunity and, being successful in that quest through their cooking skills and ability to run restaurants, made their mark on Montgomery's history. In their restaurants, Martin Luther King stopped by for his morning paper, Scott and Zelda Fitzgerald enjoyed hotdogs and Hank Williams sang his last song. The Greek restaurateurs created economic opportunity and many enjoyable meals for Montgomery's residents and guests.

ACME AND TOWN TAVERN

According to Tom Connor, in his popular *Montgomery Advertiser* column "Remember When," Pete Gallis opened the Acme Café in 1905, just off Court Square at 12 South Court Square, as a "Men-Only Café." Connor continued to say that "railroaders and farmers jammed the big horseshoe counter." On Saturday, the crowds swelled as they gathered around the radio to hear the "Grand Ole Opry" broadcast from Nashville, Tennessee. Connor said that writer Scott Fitzgerald was a frequent customer and especially enjoyed Gallis's "famous fried fruit turnovers." The Acme Café remained the "private enclave of men until 1934." Then, in 1945, Gallis partnered with Pete Stratas and changed the name of the establishment to the Town Tavern. The Town Tavern closed in the 1950s.

BUSY BEE CAFETERIA

The Original

Prior to April 1922, the Busy Bee Cafeteria operated as the Busy Bee Café. On May 20, 1916, a *Montgomery Times* advertisement invited guests to a "Big Special Sunday Dinner" for fifty cents. In addition, the promotion informed the public that "Charles' orchestra will furnish music noon and evening." A *Montgomery City Directory* advertisement gave 8 South Perry Street as the café's address and stated that its proprietor is George Pappanastos. As the dates of these advertisements suggest, Montgomery and the nation were experiencing shortages due to World War I, and these shortages often led to an increase in consumer prices. However, an advertisement flier stated that the Busy Bee "decided to cut prices to meet the demand of pre-war times." The advertisement assured customers that "the Café enjoys the distinction of being the leading café in good quality and popular prices for forty years."

The second page of the advertisement flier gave prices for breakfast, lunch, dinner and supper, which ranged from twenty-five cents to forty-five cents. The differing prices for dinner and supper provides a good segue to an explanation of the southern vernacular difference between "dinner" and "supper." Perhaps no one has done a better job of explaining the southern dining terms than beloved Alabama storyteller Kathryn Tucker Windham. Windham confidently declared, "True Southerners had supper in the evening. Dinner was what people today call lunch."[122] However, Windham elaborated, "A lunch was something you take on a picnic. So, it was breakfast, dinner and supper."[123]

A *Montgomery Advertiser* article dated April 1922 announced that, after fifteen years at 25 Commerce Street, the Busy Bee Café would reopen in a few days to serve breakfast, lunch and dinner as the Busy Bee Cafeteria. Notice that the names of the daily meals also changed. Windham maintained that this change was a more modern transformation, but, here, an earlier evolution is documented. The article announced that "with its evolution into a cafeteria, it has discarded a number of its old customs and replaced them with modern, efficient scientific methods." Perhaps the designation between "dinner" and "supper" was among those "old customs," but the article focused more on the restaurant's physical elements. For example, the space was newly remodeled and featured walls and ceilings of old ivory and silver, complimented with artistic glass wall lights and huge mirrors.

This advertisement came from the Busy Bee Café before it became a cafeteria in 1922. *Courtesy of the Landmarks Foundation.*

The kitchen also received a makeover. The *Montgomery Advertiser* article declared that the kitchen was "the epitome of sanitation and cleanliness." The restaurant's new equipment included "an electric dishwashing machine, a comprehensive refrigerating plant, a small ice plant and an artesian well that was two hundred feet deep." Change also extended to the restaurant's personnel; all of the kitchen's staffmembers were new and included "only American chefs versed in the culinary arts." In addition to the kitchen staff, the restaurant hired a new hostess, Mrs. Herbert Goldthwaite, who managed the dining room floor, gave guests personal attention and even acted "as a chaperone for parties given by the younger set."

Advertisements declared that the cafeteria served a "tasty breakfast, dainty luncheon and a delicious dinner." The establishment was open from 5:00 a.m. to 9:00 p.m., and its popularity, in addition to its availability of a "delicious, wholesome, and appetizing meal," was attributed to its "quick, quiet self-service, cheerful, comfortable surroundings and reasonable prices." However, the Busy Bee Cafeteria is no longer open.

THE CANDLELIGHT

The Candlelight restaurant stood at the top of Montgomery Street hill in Five Points—between Clayton, Montgomery and State Streets. Charles Z. Capanas, the restaurant's propriator, was originally from Thebes, Greece. The restaurant's art deco design included curved walls and block glass. Later, the restaurant became the Montgomery Press and Radio Club.

The Candlelight was known for its charcoal-broiled Kanas City steaks, barbecued and fried chicken, Italian spaghetti and Chinese dishes. The

This photo shows the close proximity of the Candlelight Restaurant to the Five Points area. *Courtesy of the Landmarks Foundation.*

restaurant served lunch and dinner. Its advertisements offered private dining rooms and "sandwiches sent out to your auto." The supper club was a favorite of the officers from Maxwell Air Force Base during World War II. The Candlelight is no longer open.

CHRIS' FAMOUS HOT DOGS

Since 1917

Chris' Hot Dogs is the oldest family-owned and -operated restaurant in Montgomery. Christopher Anastasios "Chris" Katechis (1896–1989) opened Chris' Hot Dogs on May 1, 1917. Its building at 138 Dexter Avenue was built in 1900 and was originally known as the Post Office Café and Fruit Stand because it stood next to the old post office. The building had no doors in the 1930s and 1940s. In 1940, Mr. Chris expanded the restaurant to include booths. He also raised an art deco, glass brick wall to divide the narrow space. His final design input was the round showcases, which resemble portholes, for memorabilia. According to journalist Tom

A good time to enjoy delicious food in a booth at Chris' Hot Dogs is after the lunch rush. *Author's collection.*

Owner Theo Katechis's F.D.R. shrine at Chris' Hot Dogs. *Courtesy of the* Montgomery Advertiser.

Connor, after the rennovations some customer lamented that "it'll never be the same," but Chris' remains a favorite. No major changes have been made to the restaurant's appearance since that time. One of the showcases still contains a bust of then-president Franklin D. Roosevelt. Chris' Hot Dogs is currently owned and operated by the founder's son, Theo, and Theo's son, Costas "Gus."

Although the restaurant has always welcomed guests to its cozy dining room, curb service was available until the 1960s. In his popular *Montgomery Advertiser* column "Remember When," Tom Connor mused, "At Chris' on Dexter Avenue, you were allowed to park three deep and wait for curb service to bring you a five-cent hotdog." Tom Connor also stated that, during Prohibition, bootleg booze was available at the Standard Club on Montgomery Street; when the Standard Club closed for the night, the tipsy crowd drifted to Chris' Hot Dogs, "where futile efforts were made to sober up on five-cent hotdogs. Sometimes, fights broke out, and Mr. Chris would have to call for police." Some remember that the crowd would only sober up to a certain point, because on Sunday mornings, breakfast coffee cups often contained something other than coffee. This was a city-wide practice and included patrons of the Elite Café.

Another story about libations in Montgomery involves singer-songwriter Hank Williams. Although no alcohol was served at Chris', Hank often ate hotdogs there and somehow got "a little too rowdy" (perhaps that coffee cup again); Hank was often asked to take a little break and leave the dining room. Another Hank story says that, one day, as he sat at the counter enjoying a hotdog and watching the hotdogs being grilled, he noticed a pretty woman walking by the door; he craned his head around and said, "Hey good looking!" At Chris', there are always plenty of napkins around that can be used to finish a song!

Chris' hotdogs are famous because of their special sauce. The famous chili sauce recipe is kept as a secret between "two or three living persons,"[124] according the restaurant's website. Mr. Chris created the sauce by "trial and error attempts."[125] The sauce has been shipped to Australia, Germany and Alaska. Approximately ten gallons of chili sauce is made every day. Chris' Hot Dogs also serves homemade hamburgers and cheeseburgers, a few chicken entrées, vegetable soup and chili (in the winter). Its side items include French fries, onions rings and chips. The menu is organized in an interesting manner. Guests may order a Chris' famous hotdog with mustard, onions, kraut and Chris' famous chili sauce, or they can opt for "Chris' Special Hot Dog" that is served with the same condiments but has two hotdogs in the bun. The theme continues with hamburgers: Chris' famous hamburger is served with mustard, onions, ketchup and Chris' famous chili sauce, while Chris' special hamburger is served with the same condiments but features two hamburger patties in the same bun. The menu goes on in the same vein regarding cheeseburgers: Chris' famous cheeseburger is served with mustard, onions, ketchup and Chris' famous chili sauce, while Chris' special cheeseburger is served with the same condiments but has two cheeseburger patties in the same bun. The menu includes a note that says, "Yes, we have plenty of napkins." The special (and secret) sauce may be purchased by the pint ($5.50), the quart ($10.00) or the gallon ($35.00).

Chris' Famous Hog Dogs has become an institution in Montgomery. Besides its great hotdogs, its popularity stems from its friendly service and the 1950s-style ambiance of their dining room. Chris' Famous Hot Dogs ignored the segregation laws that were in effect in Montgomery, Alabama, during the Jim Crow Era. A line in their promo explained, "Chris' hotdogs have been enjoyed by every walk of life. Chris' is a place where everyone, including young and old, rich and poor, black and white, from any country, are welcome and can all dine harmoniously in this wonderful institution." Many people remember Martin Luther King Jr. stopping by Chris' to get a morning paper. During an interview with Theo, an African American man politely interrupted and told the interviewer that he had been going to Chris' Hot Dogs since he was a little boy. He said that he worked across the street and would go over for a hotdog; he said that, for his entire adult life, he had been treated with kindness and respect at Chris'. Chris' popularity and fame continues into the modern era, and the comments on various travel and tourist websites extol the experience of dining at Chris' Hot Dogs.

To celebrate their one-hundredth anniversary in 2017, Chris' Hot Dogs threw a block party. The streets were closed to make room for a bandstand, where local bands performed; an antique car show that provided big shiny bumpers and fins for guests to "ooh," "ah" and reminisce over; and, of course, for hundreds to line up for free Chris' hotdogs. The city historical marker outside the restaurant explains that Chris' Hot Dogs "celebrated a century of serving the city its favorite hotdogs in 2017."

A number of milestones have been passed in those one hundred years. The largest hotdog order at Chris' comprised 2,600 hotdogs for the commissioning of USS *Montgomery* on September 10, 2016, in Mobile, Alabama. The previous record was 2,000 hotdogs for the 1963 campaign rally for gubernatorial candidate George Wallace.

The front door of Chris' Hot Dogs stays open during the lunch rush. *Author's collection.*

Governor George Wallace was not the only famous person who loved Chris' famous hotdogs. President Franklin Roosevelt stopped his train in Montgomery and ordered a box of hotdogs. Presidents Harry Truman, George H.W. Bush and George W. Bush also enjoyed eating Chris' hotdogs when they visited Montgomery. Movie stars Clark Gable, Tallulah Bankhead and Jimmy Stewart were also fans. Other famous frequenters of Chris' included Dr. Martin Luther King Jr., Elvis Presley and "countless sport stars and every Alabama governor since 1917." Author F. Scott Fitzgerald (*The Great Gatsby*) and his wife, Zelda Sayre Fitzgerald (a native of Montgomery), were also regular customers of Chris' Famous Hot Dogs in the 1920s.

Chris' Famous Hot Dogs is currently owned and operated by Chris' son, Theo, and grandson Kostas (Gus). Chris' Famous Hotdogs continue to be famous today. When Warren Zanes, producer and author of Tom Petty's biography, visited Montgomery in 2017 to participate in the Alabama Book Festival, he told friends in his New York neighborhood that he was going to Montgomery "to get a good hotdog."

ELITE CAFÉ

King of Seafood

The Elite, on 121 Montgomery Street, was a popular restaurant from 1910 to 1990. Guidebooks and postcards touted that the café was located "in the heart of Montgomery, Alabama's beautiful capital and center of the cultured South." The restaurant was known as the "King of Seafood" and seated 225 people, including counter service for the shopper's convenience.

The Elite's menu was about twelve inches long, and the front cover featured a scene of the dining room in a print that resembled a watercolor painting. The restaurant's appetizers offered included shrimp Arnaud, which was accompanied by a note that stated, "Used by special arrangement with Arnaud's Restaurant New Orleans." A customer favorite, shrimp Athenian, was noted as "our specialty" and was described as "whole shrimp marinated in an original Elite recipe, broiled and served with rice and seasoned butter sauce." The menu stated that trout almondine was "the Elite's most exciting dish," and it described the shrimp St. Jacques as shrimp, scallions and mushrooms sautéed in wine and butter, then blended into a creme sauce and topped with seasoned bread crumbs." Although the Napoli Italian Restaurant claimed to serve Montgomery's only spumoni ice cream, it was also offered on the Elite's dessert menu, along with the Greek pastry baklava. A folded part of the menu sent guests this message: "Regardless of the passing years and the increasing recognition, our aim remains the same: To secure the best food obtainable, prepare them with care by skilled chefs and serve them with distinction. We hope you will return to dine with us often." The message was signed, "Your Hosts, the Xides Family; Since 1911."

The restaurant's popular oysters were the center of two articles from the *Montgomery Advertiser* in January 1957—a customer discovered nineteen pearls in his oysters. In addition to the oysters and pearls, the article featured Fred L. Schaum, who was one of "the best-known traveling men in Alabama"; he represented the Hava-Tampa Cigar Company. As the articles continued, they said, "Even the best-known and best-liked traveling men have to eat, and this craving for food caused Mr. Schaum to fall into the good luck mentioned [finding the pearls]." Schaum was described as "a connoisseur of seafood," and it was said that he "liked his coffee strong and his seafood well-bred."

Schaum ordered a dish of oysters from his favorite waiter, H. Roy Cooley. The shucker, Charley Johnson, soon "undressed a dozen or so" that were then placed before Schaum "with the caskets open." As Schaum "began

The classic Elite Café sign was easily recognized. *Courtesy of the* Montgomery Advertiser.

A postcard featured the café dining room as it appeared in the 1960s. *Courtesy of the* Montgomery Advertiser.

his gustory gyrations," he discovered "particles in the oysters that defied his molars." Schaum then "shrieked and jumped six feet [and] three inches, measured by the cook." He had his hand covering his mouth, and when Cooley saw small white particles, he thought they were Schaum's teeth and almost fainted. However, Cooley recovered, offered Schaum a glass of water and inquired of his health. That is when Schaum showed him the pearls. There were nineteen of them; "one as large as a grain of corn, seven the size of English peas and the rest smaller." As news of the pearls spread, "the oyster sales' volume picked up like nobody's business." However, "nary another pearl" was ever found. Schaum considered attempting to find more: "If I can go through the last barrel, I'll have enough to retire." But his nineteen were the only ones ever discovered. And so ended what the newspaper article called "Montgomery's Worst Oyster Rush Since '47."

Known as the "King of Seafood," the Elite offered several oyster dishes aside from simple raw oysters. Some of the dishes they served included oyster Elite, oysters mornay on casserole, oysters Rockefeller and, in a southern twist, oysters in a pig blanket. They proudly declared, "We have served over a million oysters in season.

Lunch guests lined up outside of the Elite Café in this 1990 photograph. *Courtesy of the Montgomery Advertiser.*

Elite's proprietor Peter E. Xides also owned and operated the adjoining Casino Lounge and Crystal Café. Both cafés served from the same kitchen, and their clientele included legislators, debutantes and World War I soldiers. Writer Ruth Ott recalled that she and her friends would come into town for a movie and would go to the Crystal Café afterward, where they would get a special treat—a soda with a little monkey figurine hanging on the rim. The girls called them "monkey sprinkles." During the restaurant's most popular era, between 1940 and 1950, when Montgomery's formal parties and masked balls were held at a hotel ballroom or the city hall auditorium, downtown guests "would reassemble at the Elite after the dance was over and continue the revelry on into the night." Tom Connor, in his popular *Montgomery Advertiser* column "Remember When," claimed that "the really late bunch would meet early-morning risers on their way to be at hunting sites before daylight."

Singer-songwriter Hank Williams sang for the last time at the Elite on December 28, 1952. He and his wife, Billie Jean, attended an American Federation of Musicians holiday party. He sang "Jambalaya," "Cold, Cold Heart," "You Win Again" and "Lovesick Blues" to about 150 people. He died on New Year's Day while he was being driven to a performance at the Canton Memorial Auditorium in Canton, Ohio.

In his book, *Jim Crow and Me*, civil rights lawyer Solomon S. Seay Jr. told of his personal experience at the Elite Café. Seay described, "An imposing fixture at the corner of Lee and Montgomery Streets, the Elite reigned for decades as the favorite lunch spot and evening watering hole for the white establishment in legal, business and government circles."[126] Because of segregation laws, Seay was not allowed to dine at the Elite: "Often, I gazed at the attractive façade and wondered when I might have the chance to see the interior."[127]

On July 2, 1964, President Lyndon Johnson signed the Civil Rights Act of 1964, which banned segregation in restaurants and other public places. President Johnson was scheduled to sign the law into effect immediately, at 6:20 p.m. Alabama time. Seay decided that he would be the first black guest of the Elite Café, so he arrived with his wife and two small daughters at 5:30 p.m. Seay described the interior of the Elite: "The elegant interior did not disappoint—white linen tablecloths and napkins, the full complement of etiquette-ordered glasses and silverware and impeccably clad waiters."[128] Seay and his family were seated, but as time went by, they were not served. After more time had passed, Seay asked to speak to the manager and inquired of him whether he was going to serve Seay and his family. Seay said that the

This advertisement for the Casino Lounge invites guests to "join us" in the new bar that was shaped like a question mark and shown in the lower-right corner. *Courtesy of the Montgomery Advertiser.*

manager, "in a polite, matter-of-fact tone, related his understanding that the president would sign the new law at 6:20 p.m., Alabama time." He added, "We would be served at 6:20 p.m., and not one minute before."[129]

Seay and his family waited and were served. Seay's opinion of the Elite seemed to align with most: "The Elite—even with its service-only-at-the-right-time policy—exceeded my expectations."[130] The Elite closed in 1990.

JOE'S DELICATESSEN

Before World War I, Joe Piha and his family arrived in the United States from the Isle of Rhodes, Greece. Joe's Deli was first located at Five Points, at the top of Montgomery Street hill. Joe later relocated the restaurant downhill to the downtown area, and it was opened as the Varsity on Commerce Street. Then, in 1964, Joe and his wife, Ruth, moved again to East Fairview Avenue, across from Clover Theater. In 1972, Ruth died; Joe later married Vermelle, a longtime friend. Joe's Delicatessen is no longer in operation.

Joe's Delicatessen was a popular eating establishment in Cloverdale. *Courtesy of the Schaum family collection.*

Friends enjoyed catching a bite to eat and catching up on news at Joe's Deli. *Courtesy of the Schaum family collection.*

THE PICKWICK CAFÉ

The Best Things to Eat

The Pickwick Café was located just two blocks from Union Station, at the northwest corner of Bibb and Commerce Streets in an antebellum building. The large building had been used by the Confederate government as office space during the three months that Montgomery served as the capital of the Confederate States of America. In an early 1900 photograph, a large sign reads, "The Majestic Hotel," indicating that the building also housed a downtown hotel. Historian Wayne Flynt noted, "For many years, the Pickwick continued the antebellum tradition of culinary excellence."[131]

By 1900, the Pickwick Café was operated by members of the Ridolphi family, natives of Corsica who specialized in seafood; a city directory advertisement lists Fred Ridolphi as the proprietor. A newspaper article about Fred Ridolphi states that he traveled alone from Corsica to Montgomery when he was only twelve years old. At his first job, Fred had to stand on a box to reach the counter and wait on customers. The article went on to say, "From that point on, he has progressed until now—he owns and personally manages the most famous restaurant in the South, the Pickwick Café." The article explains that Ridolphi had been a naturalized citizen for many years and that "a more loyal and patriotic American could not be found." In addition to his delectable foods, it seemed Ridolphi was a popular item in his own right: It was long said that there were "so many who [went] into the Pickwick as much to shake hands and chat with him a while as to eat."

An October 26, 1912 *Montgomery Advertiser* advertisement stated that the cafeteria was open all night and promised that it had the "best things to eat." The advertisement also gave the cafeteria's convenient location, which was close to Union Station, at 103 Commerce; it listed Ridolphi as the proprietor and noted that oysters were a menu item.

In the *Montgomery City Directory*, an advertisement for the Pickwick Café featured a "Recommended by Duncan Hines" notation—restaurants across America wanted to receive this recommendation. The Duncan Hines brand was founded by a man named—not surprisingly—Duncan Hines. While making his living as a traveling salesman, he had the opportunity to eat in many restaurants. During this time, before the advent of the interstate and most chain restaurants, Duncan Hines said he enjoyed many fabulous meals on the road. In 1930, he wrote and self-published a

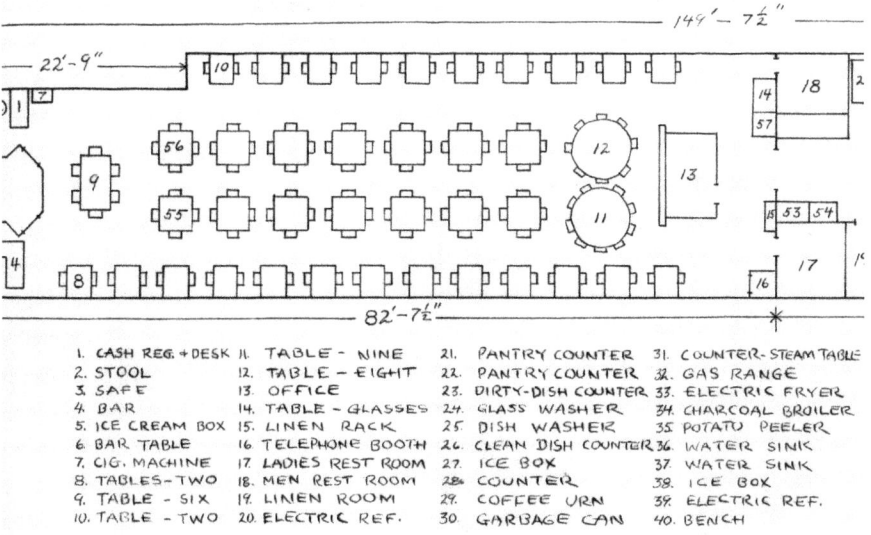

PICKWICK CAFE
MONTGOMERY, ALABAMA

1. CASH REG. + DESK	11. TABLE - NINE	21. PANTRY COUNTER	31. COUNTER - STEAM TABLE
2. STOOL	12. TABLE - EIGHT	22. PANTRY COUNTER	32. GAS RANGE
3. SAFE	13. OFFICE	23. DIRTY-DISH COUNTER	33. ELECTRIC FRYER
4. BAR	14. TABLE - GLASSES	24. GLASS WASHER	34. CHARCOAL BROILER
5. ICE CREAM BOX	15. LINEN RACK	25. DISH WASHER	35. POTATO PEELER
6. BAR TABLE	16. TELEPHONE BOOTH	26. CLEAN DISH COUNTER	36. WATER SINK
7. CIG. MACHINE	17. LADIES REST ROOM	27. ICE BOX	37. WATER SINK
8. TABLES - TWO	18. MEN REST ROOM	28. COUNTER	38. ICE BOX
9. TABLE - SIX	19. LINEN ROOM	29. COFFEE URN	39. ELECTRIC REF.
10. TABLE - TWO	20. ELECTRIC REF.	30. GARBAGE CAN	40. BENCH

The floorplan of the Pickwick Café showed some historic elements that are worth noting, including a telephone booth and a cigarette machine. *Courtesy of the Landmarks Foundation.*

guide that included a list of 167 recommended restaurants that he titled, *Adventures in Good Eating.* During this time, American families had started traveling by automobile, so they needed places to eat on long journeys. Duncan Hines's guide became so popular that his recommendation became "a nationally recognized seal of approval." His first book was so popular that he later wrote guides on a variety of regions in America. After being featured in another iconic American publication, the *Saturday Evening Post,* the popularity of Hines's guides and brand grew. This popularity in restaurant guides led to his later business in food.[132]

Historian Mary Ann Neeley wrote that the Pickwick Café "specialized in seafood" and boasted menus that included "fresh oysters and a most commendable gumbo."[133] The Pickwick menu from February 18, 1952, also features a crabmeat gumbo. The other options shown are a combination of sophisticated items and what would be called "comfort food" today. For example, guests could choose from an à la carte menu; its options included an "Arno dressing" for salads—a favorite from New Orleans.

PICKWICK
CAFE

FINE SEA FOODS

Our Specialty

Recommended by

. DUNCAN HINES

FRED RIDOLPHI, Proprietor
25 Commerce Street
Telephone 3-2162

This advertisement prominently provides the sought-after Duncan Hines recommendation. *Courtesy of the Landmarks Foundation.*

The menu's soups and cocktails included jellied tomato consomme, turtle soup with sherry and the ever-popular oysters on the half shell. The main entrées focused on a variety of meats and seafoods. The seafood options included fried oysters, tenderloin of trout and broiled Spanish mackerel. The restaurant's other main meat dishes included sirloin steak, fried chicken, roast lamb, roast turkey and broiled calf liver with bacon. Three combination meals were also available: beef stew and green beans; Spanish mackerel with french-fried potatoes and green peas; and roast lamb or pork with boiled potatoes and baked beans. All three dinners came with ice cream or Jell-O for desert. Some of the restaurant's other options for dessert included apple pie, mince pie and plum pudding with hard sauce. (A hard sauce is made from creaming butter and sugar, then adding rum, brandy or other flavoring. The sauce is often served cold over a warm desert—such as plum pudding.) It is interesting to note the contrast between beef stew and broiled Spanish mackerel, and apple pie and plum pudding with hard sauce. The prices were amazing by current standards: The first dinner combination meal only cost $0.60, the second dinner combination meal cost $1.00 and the third dinner combination cost $1.50.

In his popular *Montgomery Advertiser* column "Remember When," Tom Connor wrote that a popular offering of the Pickwick was a curbside delivery of a milkshake and a cookie. The order was brought to the car by a waiter in a white jacket for only a dime. The Pickwick Cafeteria is now closed.

Pickwick Café Arnaud Sauce

¼ cup vinegar
2 teaspoons salt
1 teaspoon sugar
1 tablespoon paprika
1 tablespoon grated horseradish
1 tablespoon creole mustard
1 tablespoon capers, chopped

Mix well, then add one-half pint of salad oil—a few drops at first, then a little at a time. Use egg beaters until thick. Put in glass jar and keep refrigerated.

Compliments of Mr. Fred Ridolphi.

THE RIVIERA RESTAURANT
AND THE MONTE CARLO LOUNGE

The Riviera Restaurant's grand opening took place on December 1, 1955, on Mobile Highway. The Riviera stood between the Continental Motel and the Saint Francis Motel. The night before the restaurant's opening, its three owners, Nick Polizos, Nick's brother Gus Polizos and the Polizos brother's cousin, Vick Fivgas, ate the restaurant's first meal: Spanish mackerel. *Montgomery Advertiser* journalist Joe Azbell called the establishment "one of the most beautiful restaurants ever constructed in this area." In the early 1960s, the Rivera Restaurant became the talk of the town when its owners organized a grand reopening after a New York decorator redesigned the dining room and the Monte Carlo Lounge was added. The Monte Carlo was a piano bar, with a small private dining room behind the lounge. In another remodel, that room was used to create a dance floor. The Monte Carlo Lounge hosted Montgomery's first oriental dancers.

The Riviera was a popular location for "Montgomery elite," local businessmen, state politicians (Governor "Big Jim" Folsom, Governor John Patterson and Governor George Wallace) and U.S. and foreign officers from Maxwell Air Force Base (General Doolittle), to gather. Celebrities, including

The Riviera opened in 1955 and was one of the most popular locations in Montgomery. *Courtesy of the Polizos Collection.*

Betty Grable and Dale Robertson, were wined and dined during their stays in Montgomery.

The restaurant served breakfast, lunch and dinner daily. The dinner menu featured seafood and steak specialties. The barbecued shrimp à la Riviera are fondly remembered, as are the broiled Riviera shish kabobs. But the restaurant's other diverse entrées included chicken chow mein and spaghetti with meat sauce. Its dessert items, all made fresh at the restaurant, included coconut, chocolate and butterscotch pies, along with shortcakes, cherry tarts and multiple favors of ice cream.

After twenty-four years of success, the opening of Interstate 65 caused the business at the restaurant to decline. Low opinions of the surrounding neighborhood also caused clientele to think twice about driving to the Riviera. Nick Polizos, the only owner left on the restaurant's closing night, said his once-loyal customers would tell him, "Nick, you're on the wrong side of town." Polizos further explained:

> *I've fought hard to keep the restaurant open. I've cut expenses. I've laid a lot of people off. I've washed dishes myself! But the money coming in wasn't enough. A lot of my customers have cried. Some loyal customers were dismayed and asked "Nick, where will we go now?" I almost cried myself. My God, I almost feel like crying now.*

The Riviera closed in 1979.

Above: *Left to right*: Nick Polizos, Vick Fivgas and Nick's brother, Gus, sharing the Riviera's first dinner the night before its grand opening. *Courtesy of the Polizos Collection.*

Left: Nick Polizos setting a table for the Riviera's last night. *Courtesy of the Polizos Collection.*

THE SHERIDAN CAFÉ

We Serve to Serve Again

John Syribeys opened the Sheridan Café on the north corner of Madison Avenue and Perry Street, across from St. John's Episcopal Church, in 1936. The café was first opened as a twenty-room hotel with a soda shop downstairs. The café was named after the World War I camp that was located north of Montgomery. Later, the soda fountain was remodeled into a restaurant, and a barbershop rented the space next door. Syribeys had previously owned a café in Corinth, Mississippi; he moved the tables and chairs from that restaurant and continued to use the same slogan. In 1937, Petro "Pete" Syribeys was a part-owner of the restaurant, and Gus Polizos worked at the café. In 1942, Gus Berdanis bought the café for $10,000. By 1944, the Polizos brothers had purchased the café. The Sheridan Café is now closed.

Notes

Two Hundred Years of Classic Restaurants

1. Neeley, *Montgomery: Capital City Corners*, 7.

Chapter 1

2. Ibid., 13.
3. Napier, "Montgomery's Railroads at War."
4. Ibid.
5. Ibid.
6. Al Bouler interview with Karren Pell.
7. Neeley, *Works of Matthew Blue*, 64.
8. Tintagel Club, *Official Guide to the City of Montgomery.*
9. Ibid.
10. Neeley, *Works of Matthew Blue*, 233.
11. Flynt, *Montgomery*, 32.
12. Rogers, *Confederate Home Front*, 149
13. Benton, *A Sense of Place*, 97.
14. *Herald.*
15. Ibid.
16. Ibid.
17. Ibid.

18. Ibid.
19. Ibid.
20. Ibid.
21. Neeley, *Works of Matthew Blue*, 48.
22. Ibid., 44.
23. Brantley, *Three Capitals*.
24. Neeley, *Works of Matthew Blue*, 94.
25. Crenshaw, *Southern Traditions*.
26. Benton, *A Sense of Place*, 228–229.
27. Sauceman, "Lane Cake."
28. Coffone, "Lane Cake."
29. Welch, *Annual Report*, 12, 4.
30. Ibid.
31. Ibid.
32. Ibid.
33. Ibid.
34. Ibid.
35. Ibid.
36. Ibid.
37. Ibid.
38. Ibid.
39. Neeley, *Works of Matthew Blue*, 53.
40. Flynt, *Montgomery*, 10.
41. Rogers, *Confederate Home Front*, 68.
42. Mary Furnald telephone interview with Karren Pell.

Chapter 2

43. Ott, "The Drive-In Era," 93.
44. MJW, "Times Gone By."
45. Singleton and Head, "The Francis Cafeteria," 91.
46. People Pill, "Georgia Gilmore."
47. Blejwas, *Story of Alabama in Fourteen Foods*, 213–14.
48. People Pill, "Georgia Gilmore."
49. Ibid.
50. Edge, *Potlikker Papers*, 20.
51. Miller, "Overlooked No More."
52. Edge, *Potlikker Papers*, 20.

53. Ibid.
54. Gingrich, "Underground Kitchen."
55. Edge, *Potlikker Papers*, 20.
56. Hawkins, *Finding Martha's Place*, 173.
57. Edge, *Potlikker Papers*, 20.
58. Blejwas, *Story of Alabama in Fourteen Foods*, 213–14.
59. Ibid.
60. Godoy, "Meet the Fearless Cook Who Fed—and Funded—the Civil Rights Movement."
61. Edge, *Potlikker Papers*, 20.
62. Turshen, *Feed the Resistance*.
63. Gingrich, "Underground Kitchen."
64. Hendrickson, "Montgomery."
65. Ibid.
66. Godoy, "Meet the Fearless Cook Who Fed—and Funded—the Civil Rights Movement."
67. Hendrickson, "Montgomery."
68. Turshen, *Feed the Resistance*.
69. Hawkins, *Finding Martha's Place*, 173.
70. Gay Harrison telephone interview with Karren Pell.
71. Hunter Harrison interview with Karren Pell.
72. Gay Harrison telephone interview with Karren Pell.
73. Hunter Harrison interview with Karren Pell.
74. Ibid.
75. Gay Harrison interview with Karren Pell.
76. Jubilee Seafood Restaurants, "About."
77. Ibid.
78. Ibid.
79. Ibid.
80. Harris, "Ben Moore Hotel," 24.
81. Ibid.
82. Hawkins, *Finding Martha's Place*, 38.
83. Ibid., 158, 175, 176, 190.
84. Ibid.
85. Ibid.
86. Ibid.
87. Ibid.
88. Ibid., ix.
89. Ibid.

90. Ibid., xii.

91. Ibid., 190.

92. Ibid.

93. Martha Hawkins interview with Karren Pell.

94. Hawkins, *Finding Martha's Place*, 158, 175, 176, 190.

95. Ibid.

96. Ibid.

97. Mary Anne Merritt interview with Karren Pell and Carole King.

98. Laurence, "Things to Know About Martin's."

99. Ibid.

100. Mary Anne Merritt interview with Karren Pell and Carole King.

101. Ibid.

102. Boswell and Walter, "Cruising the Drive-In Culture," 92.

103. Neeley, *Capital City Corners*, 121.

104. Pugh, *Heritage of Montgomery County*, 244.

105. Danna Cofer interview with Karren Pell.

106. Sinclairs Restaurants, "Cloverdale."

107. Sinclairs Restaurants, "History."

108. Ibid.

109. Sinclairs Restaurants, "History."

110. Vintage Year Restaurant and Bar, "Home."

111. Ibid.

112. Ibid.

113. Ibid.

114. Ibid.

115. Ibid.

116. Ibid.

117. Ibid.

Chapter 3

118. Sandra Polizos interview with Karren Pell and Carole King.

119. Ibid.

120. Ibid.

121. Annunciation of the Theotokos Greek Orthodox Church, "Home."

122. Windham, "Supper."

123. Ibid.

124. Chrishotdogs.com.

125. Ibd.

126. Seay, *Jim Crow and Me*, 21–22.

127. Ibid.

128. Ibid.

129. Ibid.

130. Ibid.

131. Flynt, *Montgomery*, 81.

132. Duncan Hines, "The Story of Duncan Hines."

133. Neeley, *Capital City Corners*, 71.

Bibliography

Bailey, Richard. *They Too Called Alabama Home: African American Profiles 1800–1999*. Montgomery, AL: Pyramid Publishing Inc., 1999.

Benton, Jeffrey C. *A Sense of Place*. Montgomery, AL: River City Publishing, 2001.

Blejwas, Emily. *The Story of Alabama in Fourteen Foods*. Tuscaloosa: University of Alabama Press, 2019.

Boswell, Walter D., and Barbara D. Walter. "Cruising the Drive-in Culture." In *The Heritage of Montgomery County, Alabama*. Clanton, AL: Heritage Publishing Consultants, Inc., 2001.

Bouler, Al. Interviewed by Karren Pell. Old Alabama Town. August 15, 2019.

Brantley, William H. *Three Capitals*. Tuscaloosa: University of Alabama Press, 1976.

Chris' Hot Dogs. "History." www.chrishotdogs.com.

Cofer, Danna. Interview by Karren Pell. Montgomery, AL.

Coffone, Thelma Raker. "Lane Cake: 1898 County Fair Winning Recipe." www.delishably.com.

Conner, Tom. "Sit Back, Relax and Remember When." *Montgomery Advertiser*, 1989.

Crenshaw, Annie Hadden. *Southern Traditions: Recipes and Reminiscences from Seven Generations of the Crenshaw Family*. Tallahassee, FL: Father & Son Publishing, 1998.

Dries, Marilyn Lehners. Interview by Karren Pell and Carole King. Montgomery, AL.

Driver, Michael. "Discovering the Ben Moore Hotel." www.medium.com.

Duncan Hines. "The Story of Duncan Hines." www.duncanhines.com.

Edge, John T. *The Potlikker Papers: A Food History of the Modern South*. New York: Penguin Press, 2017.

Flynt, Wayne. *Montgomery: An Illustrated History*. Albany, NY: Windsor Publications, Inc., 1980.

Furnald, Mary. Telephone interview by Karren Pell. July 12, 2019.

Gingrich, Jessica. "The Underground Kitchen that Funded the Civil Rights Movement." www.atlasobsura.com.

Godoy, Maria. "Meet the Fearless Cook who Secretly Fed—and Funded—the Civil Rights Movement." Food History and Culture. www.npr.org.

Graphy.com Editors. "Martha Hawkins Biography." www.biography.com.

Harris, Wilhelmina Howard. "Ben Moore Hotel." In *The Heritage of Montgomery County, Alabama*. Clanton, AL: Heritage Publishing Consultants, Inc., 2001.

Harrison, Gay. Telephone interview by Karren Pell. Montgomery, AL. July 8, 2019.

Harrison, Hunter. Interview by Karren Pell. Montgomery, AL. July 7, 2019.

Hawkins, Martha. *Finding Martha's Place: My Journey through Sin, Salvation, and Lots of Soul Food*. New York: Touchstone, 2001.

————. Interview by Karren Pell. Montgomery, AL. July 22, 2019.

Hendrickson, Paul. "Montgomery." *Washington Post*, July 24, 1989. www.washingtonpost.com.

Herald 26, no. 2. (Spring 2018).

Humphries, Charles. "Elite Café." www.exploringmontgomery.com.

Jubilee Seafood Restaurants. "About." www.jubileeseafoodrestaurant.com.

King, Carole. Interviewed by Karren Pell. Old Alabama Town. July 12, 2019.

Kitchen Sister. "Hidden Recipes." www.kitchensister.org.

Laurence, Haley. "Things to Know About Martin's." www.al.com.

Marriott. "Renaissance Montgomery Hotel." www.marriott.com.

Martha's Place. "About Martha." www.marthasplacebuffet.com.

McMillan, Cecil L. Blue Moon Cookbook. Montgomery, AL. 1979.

Merritt, Mary Anne. Interviewed by Karren Pell and Carole King. Martin's Restaurant. August 12, 2019.

Miller, Klancy. "Overlooked No More: Georgia Gilmore, Who Fed and Funded the Montgomery Bus Boycott." www.nytimes.com.

M.J.W., Carolyn. "Times Gone By Facebook Page." www.timesgoneby-historyofmontgomeryalblogspot.com.

Montgomery Times and *Montgomery Advertiser*. Multpiple articles. 1860–1920. www.newspapers.com/image.

Moore, Dot. Interview by Karren Pell. Montgomery, AL. July 10, 2019.

Napier, John Hawkins, III. *Essay on World War I and II Canteen*. N.d.

Neeley, Mary Ann. *Montgomery: Capital City Corners*. Charleston, SC: Arcadia Publishing, 1997.

———. *The Works of Matthew Blue*. Montgomery, AL: New South Books, 2010.

Ott, Ruth. "Downtown Montgomery: 1940s to 1960s." In *The Heritage of Montgomery County, Alabama*. Clanton, AL: Heritage Publishing Consultants Inc., 2001.

———.Telephone interview by Karren Pell. October 16, 2019.

———. "The Drive-In Era." In *The Heritage of Montgomery County, Alabama*. Clanton, AL: Heritage Publishing Consultants Inc., 2001.

People Pill. "Georgia Gilmore." www.peoplepill.com.

Polizos, Sandra. Interview by Karren Pell and Carole King. September 4, 2019.

Pugh, Mary Louise Myers. *The Heritage of Montgomery County, Alabama*. Clanton, AL: Heritage Publishing Consultants, Inc., 2001.

Rogers, William Warren, Jr. *Confederate Home Front*. Tuscaloosa: University of Alabama Press, 1999.

Sauceman, Fred. "Lane Cake." www.encyclopediaofalabama.org

Seay, Solomon S., Jr. *Jim Crow and Me*. Montgomery, AL: New South Books, 2008.

Sinclairs Restaurants. "Cloverdale." www.sinclairsrestaurants.com.

———. "History." www.sinclairsrestaurants.com.

———. "Home." www.sinclairsrestaurants.com.

Singleton, Linda Gentry, and Rod Head. "The Francis Cafeteria." In *The Heritage of Montgomery County, Alabama*. Clanton, AL: Heritage Publishing Consultants Inc., 2001.

Skopelos Project. "Home." www.theskopelosproject.com.

Tintagel Club. *Official Guide to the City of Montgomery, Alabama*. Montgomery, AL: Self-published, 1948.

Trammell, Bryan. Interview by Karren Pell and Carole King. Montgomery, AL. July 7, 2019.

Turshen, Julia. *Feed the Resistance*. San Francisco: Chronicle Books, 2017.

Vintage Year Restaurant and Bar. "Home." www.vymgm.com

Welch, Samuel W., MD. *Annual Report Alabama State Department of Health*. Montgomery, AL: 1920.

Windham, Kathryn Tucker. "Supper." www.kathryntuckerwindham.com.

About the Authors

Classic Restaurants of Montgomery is Carole King and Karren Pell's first book for The History Press. Their previous three, *Montgomery's Historic Neighborhood*, *Montgomery Then and Now* and *Images of Modern America: Montgomery*, were written for Arcadia Publishing and remain popular. Carole has been the historic properties curator for Landmarks Foundation, managing the collection at Old Alabama Town in Montgomery, for thirty years. Karren's bi-monthly live show *The Old Alabama Town Revue* features original songs and an original monolog called "Planet Karren" is in its twelfth season. Carole and Karren hope that the current residents of Montgomery enjoy learning about their history and that their books inspire increased interest and investment in historic properties.

CPSIA information can be obtained
at www.ICGtesting.com
Printed in the USA
BVHW021018270820
587463BV00015B/158